# *Courage for Today, Hope for Tomorrow*

**A Study of the Revelation**

*Revised and Expanded Edition*

ESTHER ONSTAD

COURAGE FOR TODAY, HOPE FOR TOMORROW (Revised and expanded edition)
A Study of the Revelation



Interior design: Judy Gilats/Peregrine Publications
Cover design: Terry Dugan
Cover photo: Tony Stone Worldwide

Library of Congress Cataloging-in-Publication Data

Onstad, Esther.
Courage for today, hope for tomorrow : a study of the Revelation / Esther Onstad. — Rev. and expanded ed.
p. cm.
Includes bibliographical references.
ISBN 0-8066-2651-8 (alk. paper)
1. Bible. N.T. Revelation—Commentaries. 2. Bible. N.T. Revelation—Study and teaching. I. Title.
BS2825.3.057 1993
228'.07—dc20 92-37532
CIP

The paper used in this publication meets the minimum requirements of American National Standard for Information Sciences—Permanence of Paper for Printed Library Materials, ANSI Z329.48-1984.

Manufactured in the U.S.A. AF 9-2651

97 96 95 94 93 1 2 3 4 5 6 7 8 9 10

# Contents

# Preface

Many changes have taken place in our world since the first edition of this book, but the message of the Revelation remains unchanged. God is on the throne of the universe and is in control of history. God's victory over all the forces of evil is certain. God's loving eye is on the followers of the Lamb to protect them, guide them, and see them safely home.

This book includes much of the basic material used in the first edition which has been updated with changes, additions, and deletions. I have made changes in the format of the book, placing the study questions first in each chapter, followed by a section of study helps and commentary. Hopefully, this will encourage those who study to work through the questions before proceeding to the study helps. The questions lead into the Scriptures and thus will help the learners to make discoveries on their own.

I have changed and enlarged the outline chart so that the structure of the book may be seen more clearly. One can see at a glance the perfect organization of the Revelation. It resembles a great masterpiece of music with recurring motifs building to a grand climax—in this work, it is the beautiful new heaven and the new earth.

It has been my aim to present fairly and objectively the interpretations of a number of schools of thought. This has been difficult because there is not total agreement among them. I trust that I have not made serious misrepresentations of any view.

Why another edition of this book? Because I sincerely want many people to study the Revelation, to understand its message, to discover its beauty, to be encouraged by its message of hope, and above all, to see Jesus Christ. He is the One revealed throughout the book.

It is my prayer that seeing Jesus, we will be stirred to rededicate our lives to him and follow him all the way into the beautiful city.

# Introduction

The book of Revelation to John is certainly the most neglected and misunderstood book in the Bible. Its bizarre visions of dragons, multiheaded beasts, and mysterious horses have frightened possible readers, convincing them that they would never be able to understand this mysterious writing. As a result, the Revelation has remained a closed book for many.

How unfortunate! The Revelation contains some of the most beautiful and inspiring passages in all of Scripture. It has inspired many poets, artists, and musicians. Its beautiful pictures of heaven have comforted countless sorrowing Christians. Its note of victory, especially the vision of the victorious Christ, has encouraged persecuted, suffering Christians to remain faithful to him and even to die for him should they be called to do so.

The purpose of the Revelation is to reveal Jesus Christ as the victorious Lord—alive, actively involved in his church on earth, working on behalf of his people, ultimately defeating every enemy, and coming again to establish his perfect, new world order with Christ himself as its head, and join in fellowship with his people in a beautiful new world.

With such a wonderful prospect awaiting us, we should be eager to study this book in spite of its difficulties. The Revelation does contain many difficult passages, and its symbolic language is hard to understand. But realizing that the book was written in a distinctive literary style, called *apocalyptic*, will help us to understand its message.

## CHARACTERISTICS OF APOCALYPTIC STYLE

Most forms of literature such as poetry, drama, and narrative have their own characteristic styles. Apocalyptic literature also has certain distinctive characteristics. The word *apocalyptic* comes from the Greek word *apokalypsis*, which means "disclosure," "uncovering," or "revelation." This type of literature seeks to reveal that which has been hidden. It does this through various means, one of the most common ones being the use of symbolism.

The purpose for the use of symbolism was to communicate ideas and truths to those who were accustomed to this form of writing. Because much of the symbolism in the Revelation is rooted in the Old Testament scriptures, first-century Christians were able to interpret the strange visions and symbols. But to the Roman emperors and others opposed to Christianity the bizarre language was meaningless. Thus it became a code language which helped to protect the early church from its enemies. For example, to the Christians, the vision of the multiheaded beast may have symbolized imperial Rome. They could see the meaning behind the symbol; but their opponents were unaware of the caricature.

It is very difficult for twentieth-century readers to make any sense out of the mysterious, enigmatic symbolism in the Revelation. However, we Americans have our own type of symbolism—the political cartoons found in our daily newspapers. For example, when we see a tall, thin man wearing a tall hat and dressed in clothes imprinted with the stars and stripes, we know immediately that he symbolizes the United States of America. As we encounter the many instances of symbolism in the Revelation, we will discuss them as they occur and seek to find the meaning hidden in the symbol.

As John looked into the future to the second coming of Christ, perhaps he saw things for which he did not have words to describe. If God had given him the words, what would they have meant to first-century readers or, for that matter, to people in the early twentieth century? For example, words such as *nuclear war*, *laser beams*, and *satellites* would have no meaning. John also saw spiritual realities and events that would take place before Christ's return. How could he communicate them in language that would be understood by people of every age? It was an impossible task. But God gave him the linguistic medium to use—apocalyptic language with its pictures and symbols.

The book of Revelation is like a movie being shown in living color on a wide-angle screen with four-channel stereophonic sound. The purpose of all this sound and color is to motivate us to respond so that we will not be mere spectators but will become totally involved in the drama.

Symbolic use of numbers is another characteristic of apocalyptic style. Donald Richardson and Julian Love suggest, in their commentaries, the following meaning of the numbers used in the Revelation:

- Three represents the spirit world, either the trinity of evil (the dragon and two beasts) or the Holy Trinity (Father, Son, and Holy Spirit).
- Seven is the complete or perfect number.
- Three and one-half is half of the perfect number and is therefore evil. Three and one-half years is the same as forty-two months or 1,260 days.
- Four is the number of the earth—for example, the four seasons or the four corners of the earth.
- Six is one less than seven, therefore incomplete and evil. The greatest degree of evil is found in the number *666* (Rev. 13:18).
- Ten signifies completeness and is similar to seven.
- Twelve, like seven, is considered a sacred number and signifies the people of God.
- One thousand is the symbol of highest completeness, and it occurs at least twenty times in the Revelation.[1]

The pattern for apocalyptic style came from a body of literature dated from the last two centuries B.C. and the first century A.D. These writings usually emerged during times of difficulty and persecution. Written to give courage and confidence to their readers, the messages consisted of visions announced by angels. The authors most often used pseudonyms, taking the names of well-known, Old Testament personages such as Enoch and Moses.

In contrast to these writings, the Revelation is a *Christian* apocalypse. It is the only complete book in the New Testament that uses apocalyptic style, although biblical scholars have called Mark 13 "The Little Apocalypse." In addition, passages in Matthew and 2 Thessalonians are apocalyptic in nature. The Old Testament examples of the apocalyptic style of writing are Daniel and Zechariah.

Because the Revelation is a Christian work, it differs in several respects from other apocalypses. John, its author, states several times that his book is a prophecy (Rev. 1:3; 22:7, 10, 18-19). Thus he classifies himself with the Old Testament prophets, but he uses apocalyptic style. While other apocalypses were essentially pessimistic and saw no hope for this evil world, the Revelation is optimistic. It reveals a victorious Christ who, even now, is in this world sharing his victory and promising his people a glorious future in him.

Leon Morris says:

> But clearly, he [John] has not set himself to write just another apocalypse. . . . While it has connections with apocalyptic it is yet different. It is a Christian writing setting forth what God has done in Christ and what he will do, and using something of the apocalyptic method to bring all this out. But the emphasis on the Lamb as it had been slain, i.e., on a past event of history, is both central to Revelation and absent from apocalypses.[2]

## BACKGROUND FOR UNDERSTANDING REVELATION

*Authorship.* The writer identifies himself simply as John, and nowhere does he claim to be the apostle John. The early church fathers, however, believed that the author was John the apostle, who also wrote the Gospel of John and 1, 2, and 3 John. The author states that he received the book's message while on the island of Patmos (Rev. 1:9). Irenaeus writes that the apostle John was arrested during the persecutions of the Roman Emperor Domitian and banished to the island of Patmos, where the Roman government had established a penal colony to work the mines.

Many commentators, however, do not believe that the author is John the apostle. Because the style, content, and use of Greek are so different from that of the Gospel of John, they believe that someone else named John wrote the Revelation. Regardless of who wrote the Revelation, God is ultimately the source of this book (Rev. 1:1). The message of the Revelation comes to us through John's pen.

*Date.* Tradition places the date of the Revelation in the last part of the first century, A.D. 95 or 96. This is toward the end of Emperor Domitian's reign.

*Title.* As stated, the term *apocalyptic* comes from a Greek word that means "disclosure" or "unveiling" or "revelation." The Revelation reveals Jesus Christ as we have never seen him before. When God came to earth in the person of Jesus, his glory was veiled in human flesh. But here, in the Revelation, this glory is unveiled. In the visions given to John, we see the full deity, majesty, and victory of the resurrected, glorified Lord.

Note that the Bible always uses the term *revelation* in the singular form, never the plural. "Revelations" is incorrect in referring to this book. Note how the title is written in your Bible. This book is the record of *the* revelation of the victorious Christ.

*Historical Setting*. The Revelation was written during a time of great suffering, persecution, and hardship for Christians. Emperor worship, which had been growing in the Roman Empire, reached its peak during the reign of Emperor Domitian (A.D. 81–96). Domitian demanded to be worshiped as god and to be addressed as "Lord and God." Christians and Jews who refused to do this were called atheists. Some were put to death; others were pressured socially and economically. John looks beyond the immediate persecution, however, to the persecutions that Christians will endure throughout history. The Lord's word to all suffering Christians is, "Cling to Christ! Be faithful to him even if it means death, and you will be rewarded with the victorious crown of life."

*Methods of Interpretation*. There are four main theories as to how the Revelation should be interpreted:

1. Preterist. This theory holds that the book was written exclusively for first-century Christians and is only of literary interest for succeeding generations.
2. Historical. According to this theory, the Revelation is a prophecy of all church history from its beginning to the return of Christ. Therefore, the events and predictions of the Revelation have been, and are being, fulfilled at various stages of world history.
3. Futurist. This theory considers the Revelation to be chiefly a prophecy of future events. Just as Old Testament prophets often blended present events with the immediate future and the final day of the Lord, so moderate futurists see the immediate judgments (persecutions under the beast, Rome) as a prelude to judgments at the end of the age.
4. Idealist. This theory asserts that the Revelation does not deal with *events*, but gives a symbolic portrayal of the struggles through which the church universal must pass—the struggle between good and evil. Thus the message of the book is spiritualized.

Which view shall we take in our study? Because each view has strengths and weaknesses, we need not be bound by any one of them. We know that parts of the Revelation were fulfilled in the first century, yet we will see that this book has meaning for our day and is being fulfilled even now. But this book is also eschatological in nature; that is, it speaks of the last days relating to Christ's second coming.

This study will certainly not give specific, definite answers about the end of the world. Many books on the market purport to do just that. Some writers identify China, Russia, the Common Market, and other contemporary entities in the Revelation. In 1991, during the war in the Persian Gulf, for instance, a number of books dealing with the end times were written and publishers received a great upsurge of orders for such books. These kinds of books are interesting to read and satisfy a natural curiosity about events relating to the end of the age, but they tend to interpret much of the symbolism in the Revelation literally and thus make assumptions that do not always agree with the original meaning of the text.

Christians certainly should remain alert to contemporary events and follow Jesus' injunction to watch for his return, an injunction repeated many times in his discourses. (See Matt. 24–25 and Mark 13.) But it should be remembered that God alone knows the mysteries of the end of the age. Therefore, we should approach this study with open minds and humility, refusing to allow any speculation about the end of the world to rob us of the message of hope found in this book.

Above all, we must keep our eyes on Jesus Christ! We must aim to see him throughout this book, for the Revelation is *the revelation* of Jesus Christ.

*The Message of the Book.* The purpose of the Revelation is, as mentioned previously, to bring comfort, encouragement, and hope to the church of Jesus Christ in its conflict with evil. Written to suffering, persecuted Christians in the first century, its message is for afflicted believers of all ages. The church of Christ will always be plagued by imperfections, heresies, and apostasies. It will always be persecuted and tested because there will always be a conflict between the church and the world, between Christ and Satan.

But God is *for* his people and encourages them to live faithfully in this battle between good and evil. Throughout history, God in his mercy has permitted and sent judgment on the unbelieving world in an effort to bring nonbelievers to himself. These judgments are symbolized in the Revelation by three series of judgments: the seals, the trumpets, and the bowls of wrath.

Often it seems that Satan is winning the battle between good and evil, but Christ *is* in control! When he comes to earth again, he will defeat every enemy and manifest his victory to the world. Therefore, every Christian may be filled with courage and hope, for Christ has already won the victory. That victory belongs to Christians now and will be theirs fully when they stand with their Lord in the new Jerusalem, singing the song of victory with all the saints: "Hallelujah! He is King of kings and Lord of lords."

## SUGGESTIONS FOR STUDY

1. Always begin your study of this important book with prayer, asking the Holy Spirit to enlighten you and give you insight and understanding. Ask the Lord for his promised blessing (Rev. 1:3). Expect and receive that blessing through faith.
2. Before beginning the lessons, study the outline chart of the book on page 14. This will give you a bird's-eye view of the whole book and help you become familiar with its content and structure. Note the book's four main divisions. First, the *Preparation* and the messages to the seven churches which prepare them for the coming judgments. Second, *Judgment*, in which are described the three series of judgments: the seals, the trumpets, and the bowls of wrath. Notice that each judgment is preceded by a vision of heaven. It is as though God is drawing aside heaven's curtains so that persecuted and tested believers will be encouraged to remain faithful as they view the triumphant ones singing songs of joy and victory. The third section, *Victory*, pictures the defeat of every enemy. Again we hear the glad hallelujahs because Christ has triumphed. The fourth section, *Glory*, ends the book on a joyous note with beautiful pictures of the new heaven and earth.
3. Each lesson consists of two parts—a section containing study questions and a section of study helps and commentary. To receive the most value from this study, work through the study questions first, using your Bible before you read the commentary. You will not find every question answered specifically in the study helps and commentary. That section is not an answer book. But it will give you helpful insights as you think through the questions. You may be tempted to skip the questions and read the commentary, but if you do this you will miss the challenge and blessing of

discovering insights on your own. When you need more space for answering the study questions, use separate sheets of paper or a notebook.

*Notes for Group Study*

1. If you study this book with others, you may find that each lesson is too long to be completed in one session. Each lesson may easily be divided into two or more segments.
2. If you are leading this study, try to keep the discussion related to the scripture verses being studied. The study questions will help you do this. In a study such as this on the Revelation, people may tend to get off track and spend time in irrelevant discussion. Some of this is inevitable and interesting, but try to control it.
3. Encourage group members to memorize meaningful verses and share them with the group. Use the suggestions for prayer and encourage group members to pray with one another.
4. Continue to pray that this study will be an exciting and enriching experience for you and each group member.

# OUTLINE CHART OF THE REVELATION

<table>
<tr><th colspan="4">PREPARATION</th><th colspan="10">JUDGMENT</th><th colspan="4">VICTORY</th><th colspan="2">GLORY</th></tr>
<tr><td>THE GLORIFIED CHRIST<br>1.</td><td>SEVEN CHURCHES<br>2–3.</td><td>SONG OF CREATION<br>4.</td><td>“WORTHY IS THE LAMB”<br>5.</td><td>SEVEN SEALS<br>6.</td><td>“BEHOLD A HOST”<br>7.</td><td>SEVEN TRUMPETS<br>8–9.</td><td>ANGEL AND THE BOOK<br>10.</td><td>TWO WITNESSES<br>11.</td><td>WOMAN, CHILD, DRAGON<br>12.</td><td>TWO BEASTS<br>13.</td><td>THE NEW SONG<br>14.</td><td>SONG OF MOSES AND THE LAMB<br>15.</td><td>SEVEN BOWLS<br>16.</td><td>WHORE BABYLON<br>17.</td><td>FALL OF BABYLON<br>18.</td><td>HALLELUJAH CHORUS<br>19.</td><td>SATAN ELIMINATED<br>20.</td><td>BEAUTIFUL NEW CITY<br>21.</td><td>“I AM COMING SOON”<br>22.</td></tr>
<tr><td colspan="2">MESSAGES</td><td colspan="2">SONGS IN HEAVEN</td><td>PARTIAL JUDGMENT</td><td>SONGS IN HEAVEN</td><td>MORE SEVERE JUDGMENT</td><td colspan="4">PREPARATION FOR FINAL JUDGMENT</td><td colspan="2">SONGS IN HEAVEN</td><td>FINAL JUDGMENT</td><td colspan="4">DEFEAT OF EVERY ENEMY</td><td colspan="2">HEAVEN</td></tr>
<tr><td colspan="4">1. Ephesus<br>2. Smyrna<br>3. Pergamum<br>4. Thyatira<br>5. Sardis<br>6. Philadelphia<br>7. Laodicea<br><br>God on the throne, the Lamb holds the scroll<br><br>The destiny of the world is in the hands of God and Christ</td><td>1. White horse: conquest<br>2. Red horse: war<br>3. Black horse: famine<br>4. Pale-green horse: death<br>5. Martyrs’ plea<br>6. Signs of endtimes; terror<br>7. Introduces trumpets</td><td>Interlude<br><br>Christians secure</td><td>1. Hail & fire, ⅓ earth<br>2. Volcano, ⅓ sea<br>3. Meteor, ⅓ rivers<br>4. Darkness, ⅓ light<br>5. Demonic, locusts<br>6. Demonic, horses<br>7. Introduces bowls of wrath</td><td colspan="6">Interlude<br><br>The powerful Word<br><br>Satan’s hatred of Messiah and his followers<br><br>Devil’s cohorts<br>False christ<br>False prophet<br><br>Final call to repent<br><br>Victory song of conquerors in heaven</td><td>1. On followers of the beast, foul sores<br>2. Into sea, death<br>3. Into rivers, blood<br>4. On sun, fiery heat<br>5. On throne of beast, pain<br>6. On Euphrates, demonic signs<br>7. Into air, hailstones, earthquake<br><br>“It is done”</td><td colspan="4">Babylon judged<br><br>Babylon destroyed<br><br>Hallelujah!<br>King of kings, Lord of lords!<br><br>Satan bound<br><br>Great white throne<br><br>All judged</td><td colspan="2">“Behold! I make all things new.”<br><br>Amen!<br><br>Come<br><br>Lord<br><br>Jesus!</td></tr>
<tr><td colspan="11">VISIBLE CONFLICT: WORLD VERSUS CHURCH</td><td colspan="9">UNDERLYING CAUSE: SATAN VERSUS CHRIST</td></tr>
</table>

JESUS CHRIST IS VICTOR!

# Lesson 1

## The Victorious Lord Is Alive

### REVELATION 1

You are about to begin a study of the Revelation, one of the most interesting and exciting books in the Bible.

The purpose of this study is to help you discover the meaning of this book and be truly blessed. In fact, God is so eager that the Revelation be studied that he has promised a special blessing to those who study and appropriate its message.

#### Study Questions

REV. 1:1-8: THE PROLOGUE

*Rev. 1:1-3: The Author and the Promised Blessing*

1. Read Rev. 1:1-3.
   a. Who is the real author or source of the Revelation? What difference should this make in your attitude toward studying this book?
   b. What other encouragement and motivation for studying the Revelation do you find in 1:1-3?
2. In Rev. 1:3, to whom is the blessing promised? Underline the three verbs that describe what those who are blessed do. Memorize this verse, receive the promise, and thank God for the blessings that will come to you through this study.
3. As a preparation to help you understand this book, read the Introduction on pages 6–13 if you have not already done so. Note carefully the section on apocalyptic style, which will help you understand the reason for the strange language and visions.
4. Study the outline chart of the Revelation on page 14. If you have already done so, look it over again. Try to fix in your mind the main divisions of the Revelation and a summary of its contents. Note that the book begins in chapter 1 with a vision of the glorified

Christ and concludes in chapter 22 with a vision of the new heaven and earth and a promise that Christ will come again. In between these visions, all of history is depicted.

The three series of judgments in chapters 6, 8–9, and 16 symbolize the struggle between the church and the world and between Christ and Satan and the judgment of God on the evil, unrepentant world. Before each judgment, God encourages his children by permitting them to look into heaven and see the joy and victory of those who have lived and died being faithful to Christ. Finally, we see Christ defeating every enemy and joining in fellowship with his children in the new heaven and earth.

*Rev. 1:4-5a: The Greeting*

1. Read Rev. 1:4-5a. To whom is John addressing his writing?
2. The greeting is from the Holy Trinity (vv. 4-5a). What is stated about each member of the Trinity? (The number *seven* symbolizes perfection or fullness.)
   The Father:
   The Holy Spirit:
   The Son:
3. Why do you think John uses these descriptions of God, the Holy Spirit, and Christ in his greeting? How would each description bring courage and hope to persecuted Christians living under a pagan dictator who demanded to be worshiped as god?

*Rev. 1:5b-8: The Adoration of Christ*

1. Read Rev. 1:5b-8. Underline the verbs that describe Christ's relationship with us, his children.
2. Note the tense of the verbs—past, present, and future. What is the significance of these tenses?
3. At times the early Christians must have felt insignificant compared with mighty Rome. According to Rev. 1:6, who are these Christians?
4. What encouragement would the verses about Christ and his children (5b-7) bring to suffering, first-century Christians?
5. Why would verse 8 encourage them? How does this verse affirm the fact that Jesus is true God?

## REV. 1:9-16: THE VISION OF CHRIST

1. Read Rev. 1:9-16. Where was John? (Locate the place on a map.) Why was he there? (v. 9) What happened to him there? What was he commanded to do? (v. 11) Locate these cities on a map.

   Try to put yourself in John's place—a pastor banished to a lonely island. What may have been his thoughts and feelings that Sunday morning?
2. In verse 9, how does John identify himself with the suffering Christians to whom this book is addressed? What encouragement would this bring to them?
3. In your own words, describe what John's vision of Christ (1:12-16) tells us about our exalted Lord. Which adjectives would you use to describe what he saw?
4. What do you think was the purpose of this vision? What would it mean to a small band of harried, frustrated Christians who at times were tempted to be discouraged?

## REV. 1:17-20: JOHN'S REACTION TO THE VISION

1. Read Rev. 1:17-20. What was John's reaction to what he saw? What caused him to react this way?
2. Meditate on Jesus' answer to John (vv. 17b-18). What encouragement would these words bring to suffering, first-century Christians? Memorize these verses.

## RESPONSE

1. What image or truth became most meaningful to you during this study?
2. Choose a verse (or part of a verse) from this chapter that is meaningful to you. Thank God for its truth. Keep reviewing it each day until you have memorized it.

## LESSON 1
## THE VICTORIOUS LORD IS ALIVE
## REVELATION 1

### Study Helps and Commentary

Chapter 1 introduces us to the first of several visions in the Revelation. What a beautiful vision it is! The Holy Spirit seeks to impress on our hearts that Jesus is alive, that he is in the midst of his church, and that he is all victorious. If we keep the certainties of this vision before us, we will be strengthened with courage and filled with hope to endure the coming judgments, which we will study in subsequent chapters. But before we see this glorious vision of Christ, we are introduced to the author, promised a blessing for studying this book, and given a greeting from the triune God.

### THE PROLOGUE (REV. 1:1-8)

*The Author and the Promised Blessing (1:1-3)*
God makes it clear at the beginning of this book that he is the source of the Revelation and that Jesus is the agent through whom the message came to John so that he might deliver it to the churches. This book, with its visions and prophecies of judgment and final victory, is not merely human speculation. It is in truth the word of God. Only if we realize this can we believe and trust it.

The words "what must soon take place" (v. 1) and "for the time is near" (v. 3) may raise questions as to what "soon" means. Jesus uses this word three times in Revelation 22. We do well to remember that God says this from his perspective, not ours. With him, "one day is like a thousand years, and a thousand years are like one day" (2 Peter 3:8). Perhaps another reason for these words is that they were written so that every generation will wait expectantly for the Lord. The Old Testament prophets merged the distant future with the present so that they often appeared as one. Here the seer looks down through the eons of time and tells his readers that the dawn is breaking. The Lord's return is always imminent. We may expect him at any time.

*The blessing* (v. 3) is the first of seven beatitudes in the Revelation. The promised blessing is for those who read the prophecy aloud in the congregations addressed and also for those who listen to the reading. This indicates that the book is not to be closed, but is to be read openly. This also indicates that the purpose of the Revelation is to bring a blessing that will be experienced when the message of the book is kept in the heart and heeded.

*The Greeting (1:4-5a)*

Written as a letter, this book uses the customary letter form of that day, listing the writer, the intended readers, and the salutation. The writer refers to himself simply as John, indicating that he was well known to the churches of Asia Minor. He addresses his message to the seven churches of Asia Minor. These were actual churches with which John was acquainted.

We might ask, "Why was the Revelation directed only to these seven churches?" Perhaps situations in these churches apply to churches of all ages. Also, the use of the symbolic number seven, which stands for completeness, would indicate that the message is for the church universal. Another indication that the message is meant for all who read the book is the exhortation throughout Revelation 2–3: "Let anyone who has an ear listen." The extreme futurists (dispensationalists) believe that the seven churches are not actual, historical churches but that each represents a successive stage of world history.

In this passage, John gives the usual New Testament greeting of grace and peace. The source of these blessings is the Holy Trinity. God is spoken of as the one "who is and who was and who is to come" to indicate his eternalness. He is the same yesterday, today, and forever. What a comfort to those who are going through tribulation! The God who led and preserved his people in times past will do so now and will continue to do so.

*The seven spirits.* This phrase refers to the fullness and completeness of the Holy Spirit. Note that the Holy Spirit is before God's throne. He has access to all the things of God and Christ so that he can send them to minister to us (John 16:13-14). This imagery perhaps had its source in Zechariah 4.

The greeting also comes from Jesus Christ, who is called:

*Faithful witness.* This refers to his earthly ministry and death. Jesus was the faithful, consistent witness who sealed his witness with his blood. His example would be a great encouragement to suffering Christians to be faithful, even to the point of death.

*Firstborn of the dead.* Christ's resurrection assures all believers that they, too, will be raised from the dead. What a comfort for those who were being harassed and persecuted or who might be martyred for their faith.

*Ruler of the kings of the earth.* What a comfort this was to persecuted Christians living under a Roman ruler who demanded to be worshiped as god and who appeared to be sovereign. What a comfort to all Christians living under anti-Christian governments. Jesus is the ruler of kings. At present, he is at the right hand of God, ruling the nations. When he returns to earth, his sovereignty will be revealed and all earthly rulers will fall down before him and acknowledge that he is King of kings and Lord of lords.

*The Adoration of Christ (1:5b-8)*

When John contemplates what Christ has done and will do for his people, he bursts into a doxology of praise.

*Jesus loves us.* Note the present tense of the verb. His love is constant, even during difficult, testing times when we are tempted to think that he has forgotten us.

*Jesus has freed us from our sins.* What greater proof of his love than our redemption at the price of his blood! How comforting for the early Christians, when evil was rampant and the love of God seemed obscure, to be able to look at the cross and say, "We are loved."

*We are a kingdom and priests.* All who have accepted the love of Christ and live in the forgiveness of sin are members of God's kingdom. As priests, they have free, open access to the very presence of God. When these persecuted Christians would remember who they were—"VIPs" in God's eyes—they would be strengthened to stand up to the God-defying Domitian and be faithful to Christ regardless of the cost.

*The Second Advent of Christ (1:7)*

The second coming of Christ is a great comfort to afflicted believers, for then all wrongs will be set right and righteousness and justice will rule. Those "who pierced him" are not only those who caused his death, but also all who have rejected him. They will wail when they finally realize whom they have rejected. The wailing mentioned here does not seem to imply repentance, because there is no indication in the Revelation that judgment of God's enemies causes them to repent.

*God, the Sovereign Lord of History (1:8)*
*Alpha* and *Omega* are the first and last letters of the Greek alphabet. God affirms here that he is in control of all history—its beginning, its end, and everything in between. He is eternal. He does not change. He is all powerful, the Almighty who is above every power and ruler on earth.

## THE VISION OF CHRIST (REV. 1:9-16)

Note how John identifies with his readers as being one with them in their sufferings. This statement in verse 9 seems to indicate that he had been banished to Patmos because of his faithful witness for Christ, perhaps for preaching against emperor worship. Patmos is a small island about ten miles long and five miles wide, sixty miles from Ephesus, where, according to tradition, John served as pastor. It was a bleak, rocky island where criminals were sent to work in the salt mines. They were treated cruelly and often beaten. They were given insufficient food and scanty clothing, had to sleep on the bare ground, and sometimes were made to wear chains. However, they were not kept in a prison but were free to move about with some limitations. Visitors to the island of Patmos today (the author of this study has had that privilege) are shown a cave where it is believed John wrote the Revelation.

It was Sunday morning. As John walked along the rocky coastline of this island, perhaps he was thinking about his congregation, praying for them, and longing to worship with them. But God gave him the greatest of all worship experiences!

John is "in the spirit," as William Hendricksen writes: "John's soul seems to have been liberated from the shackles of time and space. He is taken out of contact with the physical world round about him. . . . He *sees* indeed, but not with physical eyes. He *hears*, but not with physical ears. He is in direct spiritual contact with his

Savior. He is alone with God. He is wide awake and every avenue of his soul is wide open to the direct communication coming from God."[1] In this state, he hears a voice of power and authority that sounds like a trumpet. The voice instructs him to write to the seven churches of Asia Minor.

On turning to see the identity of the voice, he is granted a glorious vision of the exalted Lord. First he sees seven lampstands, perhaps in a semicircle. In the center, he sees a figure bathed in light who looks like a man but who is more than a man. His dress, indicating dignity and authority, is similar to the dress of the Old Testament priests.

*His hair, which is white as white wool*, implies deity, eternalness, and holiness. *His eyes, which are like a flame of fire*, represent Jesus' ability to penetrate the heart and unmask all sin and falsehood. Implicit here also is the idea of judgment, for when people reject the love of God, holy wrath follows.

*His feet, like burnished bronze*, bring to mind a line from the *Battle Hymn of the Republic*: "He is trampling out the vintage where the grapes of wrath are stored." It may imply the coming judgment.

*His voice* was "a roaring symphony of power perhaps like the sound of Niagara Falls."[2]

*The seven stars* may represent either a supernatural being such as an angel that is assigned to each church or the pastor of each church. These stars are in Christ's right hand. He has authority over them; he cares for them; he protects them. What an encouragement for every pastor.

*The two-edged sword that came from his mouth* is a symbol that should not be taken literally. What does it mean? In several places in Scripture, the word of God is referred to as a sword. The word of God penetrates like a sword (Heb. 4:12), and like a sword it will destroy its enemies (Isa. 11:4).

*His face was like the sun.* It is impossible to look directly into the sun without being blinded. We cannot look at an eclipse of the sun without taking proper precautions. Yet the only way John can adequately describe the dazzling glory of the exalted Christ is to compare him with the sun shining in all its strength.

John's vision of Christ is a mosaic of images from the Old Testament, especially from Daniel and Ezekiel (Dan. 7:9; 10:6; Ezek. 3:2).

If we believe, as the early church fathers did, that the author of the Revelation is the apostle John, then we know that he had been very close to Jesus during his earthly ministry. Now, John sees Jesus after his ascension and glorification. The vision of the exalted Lord causes John to fall prostrate before him. He is Jesus—robed in glorious splendor, the exalted King—coming to search out and heal his church and to bring judgment on his enemies.

The vision was not meant to frighten John, but to comfort him. How reassuring the familiar words, "Do not be afraid," must have sounded to John, who had heard them many times before from Jesus' lips. John is assured by Jesus' words that he is indeed the same Jesus who lived on earth, died, and rose again to conquer death and the grave. Jesus is indeed God in the flesh, living to conquer and coming again to judge. A loving touch from Jesus restores John's strength and confidence.

This vision would also bring comfort and courage to other Christians who were tempted to discouragement, some of whom would lose their lives for their faith. This vision would reaffirm and strengthen their faith in the living Christ. He was truly man. He knew what they were experiencing, for he, too, had suffered and died. He was also truly God and *he was alive!* In him they would be victorious, whether in life or in death.

## RESPONSE

We, too, need this vision of the exalted Lord. Too often we have focused our attention on the babe of Bethlehem or on the lowly man of Galilee. We need to recognize Jesus' authority and dignity, his holiness and purity, his majesty and power. He is the One who is coming back to judge. We need to permit his eyes, which are like a flame of fire, to penetrate our hearts and expose our sin and anything that may displease him. Each of us needs to meditate on his words, "I am alive forever and ever" (Rev. 1:18), until they strike fire in our hearts with the glad certainty that he is alive for us and that he lives in our hearts.

Ask the Holy Spirit to imprint the meaning of this vision deeply on your heart.

On my heart imprint your image,
Blessed Jesus, king of grace,
That life's troubles nor its pleasures
Ever may your work erase;
Let the clear inscription be:
Jesus, crucified for me,
Is my life, my hope's foundation,
All my glory and salvation!

Thomas H. Kingo, 1634–1703;
Tr. Peer O. Strömme, 1856–1921

# Lesson 2

# Christ Is Concerned for His Church

## REVELATION 2–3

In chapter 1, the first vision is given to John. He sees the living Lord of the church standing in the midst of seven golden lampstands, which represent the seven churches of Asia Minor. Jesus instructs John to write what he sees, "what is, and what is to take place after this" (v. 19). In Revelation 2 and 3, Jesus gives John a message for each of the seven churches. In this lesson, we will study these messages, which contain important truths that also apply to the church of our day.

### Study Questions

CHRIST'S MESSAGE TO THE SEVEN CHURCHES

Complete the material on the chart on page 26. Read the background material on pages 28–30 about the first church, Ephesus, and then read the biblical passage relating to that church. Then fill in the spaces on the chart that relate to Ephesus. Proceed to the next church and follow this procedure until you have completed the chart. You may wish to make a larger chart to have more room for writing. Note that each message follows a pattern. For some churches, there is no rebuke. For others, there is no commendation. For all, there is a promise!

CHRIST'S MESSAGE TO HIS CHURCH TODAY

1. Christ Looks for Love (Ephesus). Read Rev. 2:1-7.
   a. Of the qualities that Jesus commends, in which is the twentieth-century church the weakest?
   b. What is meant by "the love you had at first"? What causes a person to lose the glow of this first love?
   c. Why does Jesus place such high value on this love?

| Church | Christ's Title | Commendation | Rebuke | Advice and Warning | Promise |
|---|---|---|---|---|---|
| Ephesus | | | | | |
| Smyrna | | | | | |
| Pergamum | | | | | |
| Thyatira | | | | | |
| Sardis | | | | | |
| Philadelphia | | | | | |
| Laodicea | | | | | |

2. Christ Looks for Faithfulness (Smyrna). Read Rev. 2:8-11.
   a. If you knew that a time of testing and persecution was coming, when loyalty to Christ could mean suffering or death, how would you prepare your children and yourself for wholehearted allegiance to Christ?
   b. List the ways that Christianity is being threatened in our society today.
3. Christ Looks for an Uncompromising Stand for Truth (Pergamum). Read Rev. 2:12-17.
   a. How does this message to Pergamum apply to the church today?
   b. Against which doctrinal errors must today's church be on guard?
4. Christ Looks for an Uncompromising Stand Against Evil (Thyatira). Read Rev. 2:18-29.
   a. What situations do Christians face today that may tempt them to compromise their convictions?
   b. What are some practical ways by which we can take a stand against evil in our society?
5. Christ Looks for Spiritual Life (Sardis). Read Rev. 3:1-6.
   a. What are the marks of a spiritually alive person?
   b. What characterizes a spiritually alive church?
6. Christ Looks for a Vital Program of Evangelism (Philadelphia). Read Rev. 3:7-13.
   a. What opportunities for outreach are your church neglecting?

b. Recall a meaningful experience you have had when sharing your faith in Christ.

7. Christ Looks for a Burning Zeal (Laodicea). Read Rev. 3:14-22.
   a. Many people believe that of the seven churches, Laodicea is most like the church of today. Which characteristics of the Laodicean church point toward this conclusion?
   b. In your opinion, what are the marks of a lukewarm Christian?
   c. Why do you think Christ prefers that a person or church be cold or hot rather than lukewarm?
   d. How does Rev. 3:20 provide an answer for that which is lacking in the church in Laodicea and in all the churches?
8. According to Rev. 3:20, how can you be sure that Christ is living in your heart?

## OUR RESPONSE

If you are studying in a group, let each person choose one of the following prayers or use one of your own that has grown out of this study. Those who wish to do so may share their prayers audibly.

- Lord Jesus, thank you for your great love for me. Flood my heart with your love so that I may love you as I should.
- Lord, I admit that I know very little about suffering for your sake and it frightens me to think about it. Make me strong, O Lord, so that I will be true to you whatever the cost.
- O God, it's so easy to compromise my convictions and my actions because of what others say or think. Please forgive me. Help me to be bolder in my witness for you.
- O God, sometimes my spiritual life seems dead. O Holy Spirit, come and fill my heart and make me truly alive.

**LESSON 2**
**CHRIST IS CONCERNED FOR HIS CHURCH**
**REVELATION 2–3**

## Study Helps and Commentary

In Revelation 1 we saw the first vision of the book—the living, glorified Christ standing in the midst of seven golden lampstands. These lampstands represent the seven churches to which the messages in chapters 2 and 3 are addressed. In a broader sense, the lampstands represent the church of all ages, for the strengths and weaknesses that Christ points out to the churches of Asia Minor can be found in churches throughout history.

Note that each message follows a pattern. First a description of Christ is given, taken from the portrayal of Christ in the first vision (1:12-16). Each description or title tells something about Jesus, what he does or who he is, and relates in a meaningful way to the conditions in the church that Jesus addresses. Then Jesus analyzes each church, offering words of commendation, rebuke, and warning. There is no word of rebuke for the churches at Smyrna and Philadelphia and no word of commendation for the churches at Sardis (except for the few faithful ones) and Laodicea. Jesus does give each church an encouraging promise, however. In each message, he says solemnly to the Asian church and to us today, "Let anyone who has an ear listen to what the Spirit is saying to the churches."

## MESSAGE TO THE CHURCH IN EPHESUS (REV. 2:1-7)

*Historical Background*

With a population of a quarter million people, Ephesus was the most important and wealthy city in Asia Minor. It had a thriving seaport and a busy, prosperous business center. The beautiful temple of the Roman goddess Diana (Greek, Artemis), one of the Seven Wonders of the World, was also located there. This temple became the center for worship of the Roman goddess Roma and also of the Roman emperor. In it, prostitution was practiced as a part of the temple worship. Escaped criminals would flee to it for refuge. Because of its importance and wealth, Ephesus was called the "Vanity Fair of the Ancient World." Since all roads from Asia to Rome led through

Ephesus, and since Christians were brought through Ephesus to be flung to the lions in Rome, Ignatius called Ephesus the "Highway of the Martyrs."

*The Church in Ephesus*

The church in Ephesus was the most important church in the Asian province. Paul stayed there almost three years during his second missionary journey (Acts 19–20), and God greatly blessed his ministry. Although Paul may not have visited any of the other churches in Asia, the transformed lives in Ephesus touched all the surrounding regions. Timothy was put in charge of the work when Paul left, and later (about A.D. 66) the apostle John served as pastor in Ephesus.

Thirty or forty years after the church had been established, John was in exile and wrote to his former congregation. A new generation of Christians had sprung up that seemed to have lost the warm love and joy that had characterized the first congregation. Outwardly, the church at Ephesus was a model church, "a beehive of activity." It was absolutely correct in its doctrinal teachings and did not tolerate any false doctrine. The Nicolaitans, however, were a religious group that had tried to undermine the church's teachings. Information on them is obscure, but it seems that they had condoned immorality and idolatrous feasts. They had caused much grief and hardship for the church, but the Ephesian Christians had stood steadfastly against them. Jesus graciously commends the Ephesian church for its zeal and strength.

*Christ's Message to His Church Today: Christ Looks for Love*

All of these fine qualities in the Ephesian church did not fully satisfy Jesus. He seeks a warm, loving, personal relationship with his people. He is more interested in our relationship with him than in what we do for him.

In 1 Corinthians 13 we read of the importance of love. Service without love becomes drudgery. Speaking without love becomes mere noise. Taking a stand for correct doctrine without love leads to harshness, pride, self-righteousness, and legalism. Enduring hardship without love makes people bitter and rebellious. Love for Christ is the ingredient that must control and beautify all our relationships, whether they be with others, ourselves, or God.

We need to be careful, lest we become so busy with matters of the kingdom that we do not have time for the *best*—abiding in the love of Christ. When the church neglects this, it slips into a merely conventional Christianity. Unless the church repents and returns to a love for Christ that is as "fresh as morning dew," conventional Christianity will develop into "pious hypocrisy which leads to stagnation and spiritual death."[1] Because of the seriousness of this condition, Jesus warns that unless the church repents and recaptures its love of Christ, it will lose its light.

## MESSAGE TO THE CHURCH IN SMYRNA (REV. 2:8-11)

### *Historical Background*

Smyrna, a prosperous city rivaling Ephesus for prominence, was located about thirty-five miles north of Ephesus on the Aegean Sea. It possessed an excellent harbor and a large stadium that was famous for its games. Known today as Izmir, Smyrna had remained loyal to Rome and had been granted the privilege of erecting a temple for Emperor Tiberius in 20 B.C., thus becoming a center of emperor worship.

It appears that a colony of Jews in Smyrna sided with the Gentiles and the Roman authorities in harassing and persecuting Christians. Some years later (A.D. 155), this group caused the martyrdom of Polycarp, the bishop of the church in Smyrna.

### *The Church in Smyrna*

We have no record of how the church in Smyrna was founded. If not developed by Paul, then perhaps it developed as a result of his ministry in Ephesus. The Christians in Smyrna had few material goods. It was a real sacrifice to be a Christian there. Often, as a result of their faith, Christians lost their jobs and their property was confiscated. They were also imprisoned and falsely accused by the Jews before Roman tribunals. These Jews, who prided themselves in their religion and their synagogue, had departed so far from the true meaning of their faith that they had aligned themselves with those who practiced emperor worship. They denied Christ and hated the Christians. Thus, instead of being a synagogue of God, their synagogue was in reality a synagogue of Satan.

Jesus begins his message to this church with comforting words, "I know." He is fully aware of their poverty, persecution, and harassment; he had experienced the same. But he does not give the Christians there any opportunity to feel sorry for themselves. "You are rich in me," he says in effect. He assures them that their suffering will be brief, especially so in the light of eternity, and that he is in control of this period of time. The ten days mentioned here are not to be taken literally; they symbolize a short, controlled period of time.

Jesus' message would encourage the Christians to be faithful during the persecutions, which were a great test of their faith. Jesus tells them that if they remain loyal to him, even to the point of giving their lives, he will give them "the crown of life."

In Smyrna, which was famous for its games, winners received garlands or wreaths. Jesus is saying, "Be true to me. Do not deny me, regardless of the cost, and I will give you a victor's wreath that doesn't fade: eternal life with me." And if they should die for his sake, they would not experience the "second death," which refers to eternal death—separation from Christ. Jesus gives no rebuke to the Smyrnian church.

*Christ's Message to His Church Today: Christ Looks for Faithfulness*

Responsible observers note that there have been more martyrs for the Christian faith during the twentieth century than during the nineteen hundred years that preceded it. Fascist and communist governments have repeatedly sought to crush the Christian church. Countless Christians have been imprisoned or put to death. All of this manifests Satan's hatred of Christ.

Can our country hope to escape God's judgment if it blatantly continues to disobey God's laws and does not repent? Ruth Graham has said that if God does not send judgment on America, he will have to apologize to Sodom and Gomorrah. If suffering should come, would we be able to endure victoriously for Christ? How can we prepare for such an eventuality? Here are some suggestions from *World in Revolt* by M. Basilea Schlink, who lived through the Hitler regime:

1. We must be completely dedicated to the will of God.

2. We must resist the advance of the enemy by praying and wrestling for every person who is threatened so that people may be freed from the trap [of the devil].
3. We must make a clear decision for Christ and stand against a theology that abandons the substance of the word of God.
4. We must take our stand for Jesus and be willing to be scorned and called old-fashioned by refusing to compromise.
5. We must overcome fear by learning to trust God in everything, in both small and large matters.
6. We must be willing to give up everything that is of value to us, even the most precious things, if Jesus calls us to do it. Whoever does not learn to trust the Father, in all matters large and small today, will despair when the time of catastrophe sets in.[2]

Are we willing to face the possibility of suffering for Christ's sake? Are we willing to prepare for it?

## MESSAGE TO THE CHURCH IN PERGAMUM (REV. 2:12-17)

### *Historical Background*

Pergamum, located about fifty-five miles north of Smyrna, was perhaps the most impressive of the seven cities. It boasted a library of 200,000 parchment scrolls. The word *parchment* (Latin *pergamena*) derived its name from this city because parchment was first obtained in Pergamum. The city also contained many temples dedicated to Roman deities. A huge white marble altar dedicated to Zeus, built on a hill one thousand feet high, was one of the Seven Wonders of the Ancient World. Pergamum also boasted a temple to the god of healing, Askelepias. People from throughout Asia came to Pergamum for healing. It was a modern Lourdes.

There were two main religious cults in Pergamum: the cult of emperor worship, of which Pergamum was the headquarters; and the worship of Askelepias. Refusal to worship the emperor was considered treason. Satan was behind these false religions. He was so influential through these cults that his throne was said to be in Pergamum.

### *The Church in Pergamum*

Jesus tells the Christians in Pergamum that he is aware of the difficult place in which they live. He knows the pressures they face to worship the emperor by sprinkling a little incense before his image and saying, "*Kyrios Kaisar*" (Caesar is Lord). He knows they comprise a small, insignificant group that is looked down upon by the elite because they worship the lowly Nazarene. Jesus commends them for remaining true to him in spite of these difficult circumstances.

Many Pergamese Christians had come out of paganism, so the temptation to give up Christ and return to their old religions must have been very keen. But they had remained faithful to Christ, even when one of their number, Antipas, had been put to death for his faith. This is the only information we have about him. Note Jesus' beautiful commendation of Antipas: "My witness, my faithful one." The Greek word used here for witness is *martys*, from which comes the English word *martyr*.

Although these Christians, as a whole, had been faithful to Christ, Jesus rebukes them because they had permitted people who believed false doctrine to remain in the fellowship. Because the church tolerated impure doctrine, it was being influenced by pagan morals. The account of Balaam (Num. 22–25; 31:16) refers to any person or group that compromises with the immorality and idolatry of paganism.

The Christians in Pergamum were tempted to take part in the heathen feasts and perhaps even to practice immorality, which was an accepted part of the pagan temple worship. Perhaps some of the Christians were tempted to compromise their faith by sprinkling a little incense before an image of the emperor, thinking it wasn't such a serious matter because they really didn't mean it; in their hearts they knew that Christ was Lord. But Jesus tells them they must take a stand; they are not to tolerate evil or make a compromise with evil. The church must exercise discipline and exclude those who believe false doctrine until they confess their error. The whole church must repent of its laxness or else Jesus himself will bring judgment on the church. He promises those who resist these false teachings that they will feast with him in glory.

The *white stone* has been given various interpretations. It could symbolize victory, free citizenship in the kingdom of God, justification, or an eternal friendship with Christ.

*Christ's Message to His Church Today: Christ Looks for an Uncompromising Stand for Truth*

The false religions that threatened the faith of Christians in Pergamum find their counterparts in occultic religious movements today. These include astrology, fortune telling, spiritualism, witchcraft (also known as wicca), and many others. The Bible warns against them (Isa. 47:10-15, Deut. 18:10-12). The god of these religions is not the personal God whom Christians love and worship, but rather an impersonal force like that in the *Star Wars* movies. The fact of sin is not recognized, and wrongdoing is labelled as ignorance or mistakes. Thus there is no need for forgiveness or a Savior.

Also of great concern to many Christians is the fact that in some quarters of the church the basic doctrines of the faith are being questioned: the virgin birth, the deity of Christ, and his bodily resurrection.

To counteract the dangers of any false teachings, the church needs to increase its Bible study programs and place special emphasis on the basic doctrines of the Christian faith. Doing this will equip its members not only to withstand attacks on their beliefs and give them discernment to detect error, but will also enable them to help others who are floundering in their search for truth.

## MESSAGE TO THE CHURCH IN THYATIRA (REV. 2:18-29)

*Historical Background*

The city of Thyatira was the least important of the seven cities. However, it was a thriving trade center that had many trade guilds for potters, cobblers, tanners, weavers, and so on. Lydia, whom Paul met in Philippi, was a businesswoman from Thyatira. She obtained the famous, purple-dyed wool in Thyatira and sold it in Philippi. Perhaps she was a representative of the dyers' guild.

Each trade guild had its god. This presented a difficult problem for the Christians. If they wanted to hold a job, they were expected to be members of a trade guild and attend its festival. This would include a feast at which food that had been offered to the guild god was served. Following the feast, there was usually much revelry and immorality. If Christians refused to join a guild, they jeopardized their jobs. If they walked out on the wild party, they were ridiculed and persecuted.

*The Church in Thyatira*

We do not know who founded the church in Thyatira, but after Lydia became a Christian through Paul's ministry and returned to Thyatira on a business trip, she was eager to tell of her newfound faith. Now she was on the King's business. Perhaps, through her witness, many came to know her Lord. These new Christians may have formed the nucleus of the church in Thyatira, which was growing in the Lord. The Christians there were working, loving, and faithfully enduring. Jesus gave this church a finer commendation than he gave to the church in Ephesus, for Thyatira was motivated by love. But, as in Pergamum, this church tolerated evil in its midst.

In the Old Testament, Jezebel was the foreign wife of King Ahab. She persuaded her husband to build a temple to Baal, thus corrupting Israel's worship of the true God. Her name symbolizes seduction to idolatry and immorality. The Jezebel referred to in Rev. 2:20 evidently was a woman in the church who claimed to be a prophetess and to have received special revelations from God. This, she said, gave her the authority to teach and advise the Christians. Perhaps she told them that she had the answer to their dilemma as to whether they should drop out of the guilds, lose their jobs, and suffer hunger and persecution, or remain in the guilds and take part in pagan activities. Perhaps she counseled them to stay in the guilds and take part in the feasts and immoralities in order to become stronger Christians. "In fact," she may have said, "if you're really going to be able to fight sin, you've got to experience it." (This was the basic philosophy of the Nicolaitans and the Gnostics. They contended that all matter was evil; only the spirit was good. So one could sin as much as one pleased with the body because sin could not touch the soul.) Perhaps Jezebel claimed that her revelations were the "deep things of God." But Jesus labels her teaching as the "deep things of Satan."

The Christians in Thyatira were aware of this woman and her false teachings in their midst, but they did nothing about it. This was their sin. Jesus graciously had given her time to repent. He warned that if she refused to repent, she would be stricken with illness and that her spiritual children who had heeded her teachings and committed spiritual adultery would suffer the same fate—spiritual death. Evidently, some people were struggling with her teachings and had not fully become her "children," so their judgment would not be as severe. They would suffer persecution unless they repented. The news of this judgment at Thyatira would spread to surrounding churches and would warn them that Christ was aware of anything they were harboring that was contrary to his spirit.

Jesus concludes this message with a gracious promise for those who are willing to pay the price of living holy, separated lives. They will share Christ's rule in heaven and will be given Christ himself, the morning star. They will share his authority and glory.

*Christ's Message to His Church Today: Christ Looks for an Uncompromising Stand Against Evil*

A church today may appear to be successful and growing, like the church in Thyatira. But like that church, it, too, may be infected with the spirit of the world. One of the dangers facing the church today is the temptation to be influenced by current, non-Christian ideas relating to morality, sex, and other controversial issues. Someone has likened the church to a ship sailing in the ocean. As long as the ship is in the ocean, it can fulfill its function. But if the ocean gets into the ship, it will mean disaster. Likewise, if the spirit of the non-Christian world floods the church, it will sink. As William Barclay puts it, "If this happens, the church will become a kind of cultured, pleasant paganism."[3]

Recently several mainline denominations have attempted to draft statements on sexuality that would be acceptable to their constituents. One such statement, rejected by its church body in 1991, was so controversial that had it passed, as one observer stated, "The church would more closely resemble a Canaanite fertility cult than a Christian church."

Jesus is warning the church today that unless it responds firmly against all forms of sin, there will be judgment. Are we standing firmly against that which the word of God declares is sin, or are our views being conditioned by the influence of the world?

## MESSAGE TO THE CHURCH IN SARDIS (REV. 3:1-6)

*Historical Background*

Sardis at one time had been one of the greatest cities in the world, but at the time of the Revelation was basking lazily in past glory. It was famous for its wool and, according to some authorities, wool dying was invented there. Located high on a mountain, the city was almost inaccessible. Because it considered itself to be impregnable and had failed to keep watch, it had been captured twice in surprise attacks. The people of Sardis were characterized by a love of ease, luxury, wealth, and profligacy, and they zealously promoted emperor worship.

*The Church in Sardis*

This church had a good reputation and outwardly had all the marks of an actively alive church. But Jesus' verdict was that the church was dead. Perhaps it had all the forms of church life—worship, prayer, service—but these were but empty shells. There seemed to be no heresy in the church, no persecution, and no suffering. It was so dead that there was no reason to attack it. It was so lifeless that the community paid no attention to it. Most of its members were nominal Christians, outwardly religious but with no inner spiritual reality.

As Jesus looks through this church's facade, he does not find any of its works to be perfect—that is, complete or adequate. The works of the church are empty because they are not motivated by the Holy Spirit. The description Jesus uses for himself in addressing this church assures the members that he has the fullness of the Holy Spirit and is able to fill their empty forms with spiritual reality. He warns them that unless they repent, wake up to their condition, confess their hypocrisy, and ask the Holy Spirit to fill them, the lights in their lampstand will go out. He will come unexpectedly, and they will lose out because they are not prepared. People in Sardis knew the cost of not being watchful. Jesus gives no commendation to this church, except to the few faithful ones who are alive in Christ and shine as lights in the darkness. Jesus knows their names, and concludes his message with a gracious promise of their future in glory.

*Christ's Message to His Church Today: Christ Looks for Spiritual Life*

"You are dead," Jesus says. What a tragic indictment against a church that seemed to be so successful and had a reputation for being spiritually alive. As Jesus walks in the midst of the church today, does he find outward forms that are devoid of inner meaning?

As we sing the liturgy and the great hymns of the faith, are we mouthing the words or are we truly worshiping? Are we *praying* the Lord's Prayer or *saying* it? Martin Luther said, "The Lord's Prayer is the greatest martyr on earth." But are we to discard these forms because they seem empty? No, Jesus tells us. We are to fill them full of meaning. If we confess our emptiness and our need for renewal and ask the Holy Spirit to fill us with himself, we will discover new life and joy and a meaningful experience in our worship and service.

## MESSAGE TO THE CHURCH IN PHILADELPHIA (REV. 3:7-13)

### *Historical Background*

Philadelphia, the youngest of the seven cities, had been founded for the purpose of spreading Greek culture and language to Lydia and Phrygia. This city was completely destroyed by an earthquake in A.D. 17. Because shocks continued to shake the city, many people moved out. Others stayed because of the good soil for growing grapes. They eventually rebuilt the city. William Ramsey says of Philadelphia, "It was the center for the diffusion of Greek language and letters in a peaceful land and by peaceful means."[4] Jesus uses this bit of history when he says to the church in Philadelphia, "I have set before you an open door" for the diffusion of the gospel.

### *The Church in Philadelphia*

Jesus gives the tenderest and the highest praise to this church. He finds nothing for which to rebuke it. The church may have been small with few resources (little power), but it had remained faithful to Christ. The problem for the Christians here was not pagan authorities who demanded emperor worship; it was Jews who had rejected Christ and therefore hated Christians because they proclaimed Jesus as the Messiah. For the second time in these letters, Jesus refers to these unbelieving Jews as "the synagogue of Satan." Through them, the devil was pouring out his venom on the Christians.

*The open door* may refer to the fact that Christians have the door into the kingdom. Christ himself said, "I am the door." This door may refer to opportunities this church had to witness to hostile Jews.

Some Jews would later respond (bow down) and confess Jesus as their Messiah. But some who had rejected Christ would persecute the Christians. Jesus promises that he will keep his faithful ones "from the hour of trial." This trial may mean an impending persecution, or it may refer to the severe persecution of Christians just prior to Christ's return. In any case, he will sustain them and give them strength to be faithful. The promise of his coming will bring them comfort and encouragement. The Christians at Philadelphia had been weak and insignificant in the eyes of the world. Because of the earthquakes, they had to move often. Because of the persecutions, they had to suffer much. But Jesus promises that, once inside the heavenly home, they will be pillars, symbols of strength and security. There will be no more moving. Christ will write his name on them, denoting his ownership. They will be his forever!

*Christ's Message to His Church Today: Christ Looks for a Vital Program of Evangelism*

God has placed many open doors before the church, and it has gone through them into missions overseas and at home. It has not only brought the gospel of salvation but also food and programs relating to health, education, agriculture, and other areas that better the quality of life. Millions of people worldwide have been touched with the gospel through the doors of Christian radio and television. The recent crumbling of geographical and cultural walls presents new opportunities to bring the word of God to people who have been deprived of it. The church must keep alert and be ready to go through these doors of opportunity while they are open, for they may close again. Christians must give generously so that there will be enough money to send Bibles and Christian workers through these open doors.

Jesus' words to the church today are, "Work while it is day. The night comes when no one can work." All of us need to confess our complacency and ask God to stir our hearts with urgency and love to share Christ with those who may not know him.

## MESSAGE TO THE CHURCH IN LAODICEA (REV. 3:14-22)

*Historical Background*

The last of the seven cities, Laodicea, was undoubtedly first in its own eyes. Laodicea was the home of millionaires, which is evidenced by the fact that when in A.D. 60 an earthquake destroyed it, its leaders refused financial aid from the government to assist in rebuilding the city. It was a wealthy commercial center, located strategically where three main highways converged. It was famous for black carpets and garments woven from the soft wool of black sheep. Laodicea was a banking center, and it is said that Cicero transacted his business there. Near the city were medicinal hot springs, and a medical school in the city had developed a remedy for weak eyes. Laodicea also boasted a gymnasium equipped with baths.

*The Church in Laodicea*

It is thought, from Paul's reference to Laodicea in Col. 4:12-16, that the church was founded by Epaphras, one of Paul's converts in Ephesus. Paul evidently wrote a letter to Laodicea from Rome (Col. 4:16), but the letter has been lost.

Of all the seven churches, Jesus condemns this one most severely. He gives not one word of praise. In Sardis, at least a few had remained faithful, but here the whole church comes under the rebuke of Christ. This church existed in an affluent society and evidently was very prosperous and self-sufficient, since its members were active in the community. Outwardly this church seemed to be in good condition and highly respected.

Christ mentions no heresies or sins, but his severe indictment is that the church is neither cold nor hot. In the Greek, these words mean *freezing* and *boiling*. The church members had not openly rejected the gospel; they listened, but there was only complacency and a half-hearted response. There was no zeal, warmth, ardor, or enthusiasm. They were lukewarm. Nowhere else in the Bible does Jesus express disgust as he does here because of their spiritual condition. No one is more difficult to win to Christ than the person who is self-satisfied, complacent, and blind to his or her condition. It is easier to win those who are "cold," who have never been touched by the gospel. Jesus said that prostitutes and tax collectors would come into the kingdom before the proud, religious Pharisees (Matt. 21:31).

Notice the words that Jesus uses to describe this church, which is so proud, complacent, smug, and self-satisfied. "You are wretched, pitiable, poor, blind, and naked," he says. In spite of their woolen garments, eye salve, and banks, they were spiritually bankrupt. Jesus loves this church as much as the others and gives its members loving counsel as to how they can secure spiritual clothing, sight, and wealth from him. There are two steps to their recovery: repentance (Rev. 3:19) and faith (Rev. 3:20). These verses spell hope, not only for the Laodicean church but also for every church or individual who is in a spiritual stupor. To those who respond and permit Christ to come in and make them alive and rich in him, he promises victory.

*Christ's Message to His Church Today: Christ Looks for a Burning Zeal*

The church today faces the same problems and temptations as the Laodicean church. We, too, live in an affluent society. We have beautiful buildings, efficient organizations, and successful congregations. However, during times of recession, many churches struggle to keep afloat. Regardless of the situation, we, too, risk becoming lukewarm and complacent. The remedy is to follow the two steps Jesus outlines to the Laodicean church: to repent and to give Jesus Christ full access to our hearts.

When we face ourselves in the light of Christ's penetrating examination, admit his diagnosis, are open and honest about our self-sufficiency and lukewarmness, and repent, we are ready to receive greater blessings. When we invite Christ to take control of our lives and make the word and prayer the center of our individual and church lives, he will change us from lukewarm Christians into zealous, empowered servants.

Rise up, O church of God!*
Have done with lesser things;
Give heart and soul and mind and strength
To serve the King of kings.

William P. Merrill, 1867–1954

*Adapted. Author changed "men of God" to "church of God."

# Lesson 3

# Christ Holds the World's Destiny in His Hands

## REVELATION 4–5

Consult the outline chart on page 14 and note how Revelation 1–5 serves to prepare God's people for the judgments that follow. Review the first two lessons with the following questions in mind:

a. How does chapter 1 serve as a preparation?
b. What encouragement for the suffering children of God is found in chapter 1?
c. How do chapters 2 and 3 prepare the church to be steadfast and victorious during persecution and judgment?

Chapters 4 and 5 give added encouragement and hope as the curtain of heaven is drawn aside. The persecuted children of God are permitted to see God in glory on the throne of the universe and Jesus the Lamb in perfect control of the world's destiny.

Read chapters 4 and 5 to gain general impressions. Try to capture the mood of these chapters. What do you see? What do you hear? Which emotions do you experience? What, in your opinion, is the focal point of chapter 4? of chapter 5?

### Study Questions

### REVELATION 4:
### GOD IS ON THE THRONE OF THE UNIVERSE

1. As John looks into heaven, he sees "one" seated on a throne. God is not described, but he "looks like. . . ." How are God's glory and power symbolized in verses 3 and 5?
2. Read Rev. 4:4-8. Try to reconstruct in your mind what John saw.
   a. At the center is a throne. Who surrounds the throne? Who are these people?
   b. What is in front of the throne?

c. Who is on each side of the throne? What do they represent? (See the study helps and commentary for this lesson.)

3. Read Rev. 4:9-11. According to the song, why is God worthy to be praised?
4. Be quiet for a few moments. Close your eyes. Visualize the scene before John: a throne in heaven, and on it the God of the universe, resplendent in glory, radiance, beauty, power, and holiness. Listen to the glorious music of the company of heaven as they sing the song of creation to the One upon the throne. Take your place among them. Worship and adore your God.
5. With this vision before your heart, sing this stanza from the familiar hymn by Reginald Heber:

   Holy, holy, holy! All the saints adore thee,
   Casting down their golden crowns around the glassy sea;
   Cherubim and seraphim falling down before thee,
   Which wert and art and evermore shalt be.
6. What do you suppose this vision meant to the Christians of John's day? Recall that they lived under Emperor Domitian who also was surrounded by great splendor and demanded to be worshiped as God.

## REVELATION 5: THE WORLD'S DESTINY IS IN THE HANDS OF THE LAMB

1. Chapters 4 and 5 are a unit and present one vision. What does chapter 5 add to the scene revealed to John in heaven?
2. Read Rev. 5:1-5.
   a. Summarize the meaning of the scroll in the hands of the Father.
   b. What caused John such great sorrow?
   c. What comfort did one of the elders give him?
3. Read Rev. 5:6-10.
   a. What do you think the symbolic descriptions of the Lamb mean?
   b. What happens when the Lamb takes the scroll from the hand of God?
   c. According to the song in verses 9 and 10, why is the Lamb worthy to be praised?

d. Usually a lion is the symbol of strength. What is the significance of Jesus being pictured as a lamb in the Revelation?

4. Read Rev. 5:11-14. Another group of singers that encircles the throne is introduced.
   a. Who are they? How many are there?
   b. Underline in your Bible the sevenfold honor ascribed to the Lamb in their song (v. 12). What is the significance of the fact that seven words are mentioned?
   c. In verse 13, the group is enlarged even more. What do these added singers represent?
   d. If you can, listen to a recording of "Worthy Is the Lamb" and "Amen" from the *Messiah*. As you listen, visualize the glory and beauty of this heavenly scene. Thank Jesus—the Lamb—for what he has done for you. Worship him.

YOUR RESPONSE

1. Think about the message of these two chapters. How can you relate this message today to people you know who are worried and fearful because of the many serious situations in our troubled world?
2. Use the message of these chapters to enrich your worship experience. As you take part in a worship service, visualize the throng of worshipers in heaven and join them in their worship of the Lamb. This is especially meaningful during the service of Holy Communion in liturgical churches.

## LESSON 3
## CHRIST HOLDS THE WORLD'S DESTINY IN HIS HANDS
## REVELATION 4–5

### Study Helps and Commentary

In the first vision (Rev. 1), we saw the exalted, glorified Lord standing in the midst of his church, encouraging, exhorting, and warning. In Revelation 4 and 5, the second vision is revealed. The scene shifts from earth to heaven, and we see God on the throne of the universe and Jesus the Lamb holding the scroll of destiny. As this scroll is unrolled in succeeding chapters, we see the intense struggle unfolding between the church and the world, between Christ and Satan. We see God's judgments on all who reject him and the final consummation of the kingdom of God. The visions in these first chapters are meant to give confidence and courage to the tried and tested people of God so that they will remain faithful to their Lord.

## GOD IS ON THE THRONE OF THE UNIVERSE (REVELATION 4)

Again John is in the spirit, not seeing with physical eyes and not hearing with physical ears. A door is opened so that John in his ecstatic state is able to see all the glory and beauty of heaven. He recognizes that the voice calling him to behold this second vision is the same voice that spoke to him before.

The first thing that meets John's eye is *the throne*, the symbol of power and authority. He does not identify the One on the throne, but from what he sees he knows it is God the Father. The reflections of light from the precious stones, the thunder, and the lightning symbolize the brilliant radiance of God's glory and majesty. Some interpreters have seen meaning in the colors of the gems. Some believe the translucent beauty of the jasper (the diamond) indicates God's holiness, the brilliant red of the carnelian indicates his judgment, and the green in the rainbow indicates his mercy and his faithfulness to keep his promises.

John sees groups of attendants surrounding the throne. The first he sees are the *twenty-four elders*. Many interpreters believe this group represents all the redeemed—both Old and New Testament saints—and that the number twenty-four symbolizes the twelve tribes of Israel plus the twelve apostles. Seated on thrones the elders are dressed in white (symbolic of Christ's righteousness) and wear golden crowns. Their struggles are over, and now they are victors rejoicing in the presence of God. Another interpretation holds that the twenty-four elders are angels, near the throne of God, ready to do his bidding. Another view is that they are New Testament Christians who have been "caught up" to be with the Lord.

Some who interpret the Revelation very literally believe that there are two phases to Christ's second coming: he comes first to gather his church, and later to judge. This view holds that the words to John, "Come up here" (Rev. 4:1), refer to the "rapture" of the church when all believers are taken up to be with the Lord. According to this view, everything from chapter 4 to the end of the Revelation is in the future; thus, Christians will not go through any judgments. This theory is known as the "pretribulation rapture." However, the words "*Come up here*" are directed specifically to John and do not refer to the church. George Ladd says, "The entire question of a so-called 'pretribulation rapture' is an assumption which does not command the support of explicit exegesis of the New Testament."[1]

*The seven torches* in front of the throne (Rev. 4:5) have the same meaning as the seven spirits mentioned in Revelation 1. They represent the Holy Spirit in all his fullness.

*The sea of glass, like crystal,* which is in front of the throne (Rev. 4:6a), reminds us of Old Testament imagery and the vision of God given to Moses and Aaron in Exod. 24:10: "Under his feet there was something like a pavement of sapphire stone, like the very heaven for clearness." This transparent, crystalline expanse before the throne would pick up and reflect the glowing colors of the stones, the gold, and the lights, and thus symbolically enhance the beauty and glory of this heavenly scene.

*Four living creatures* stand on each side of the throne (Rev. 4:6b-8). Bible scholars generally believe these creatures represent the cherubim, the highest order of heavenly beings. This symbolism is much like that found in the visions of Isaiah 6 and Ezekiel 1. The eyes in front and behind and the wings full of eyes symbolize their all-seeing intelligence, swiftness, and readiness to serve and carry out the will of God. Their four different likenesses—lion, ox, human, and eagle—may represent all of God's creation. They may symbolize everything that is noblest, strongest, wisest, and swiftest in nature.

The four living creatures sing day and night of the holiness and eternalness of God. "Holy, holy, holy, the Lord God the Almighty," they sing. The phrase "*is to come*" (v. 8b) may express the longing of creation to be set free from its bondage to decay, for when Christ comes again, all of nature will be released from its bondage (Rom. 8:19-22).

Whenever the living creatures sing out their glory and honor and thanks to God who is on the throne, the twenty-four elders join them. They fall down in humility, casting their golden crowns before the throne, acknowledging that their victory, joy, and blessedness have come from the hand of God. Their song is the song of creation, affirming that the sovereign will of God is behind everything that exists.

*Reassurance for Discouraged Christians*

The purpose of this vision was to draw the eyes of discouraged Christians upward to the throne room of heaven to behold the King of the universe seated in radiant splendor, surrounded by his court of worshiping, adoring attendants. What earthly monarch could claim such magnificence? The boasted greatness of Emperor Domitian would pale in comparison. A royal procession chanted the very words *"You are worthy, our Lord and God"* when Domitian made his entrance. Early Christians would easily make the connection, for here was One seated above the earth who alone was worthy of praise. He alone possessed all power, although at times to the harassed Christian it may have seemed that the power of Rome was supreme. Here was the Lord God, the Creator of all things, even of every emperor—including Domitian. Therefore, O fainthearted Christians, lift up your hearts! Behold your sovereign God. He rules the world from his throne in heaven. He is in perfect control. When earthly rulers boast and strut and make ambitious plans to outwit God, "He who sits in the heavens laughs" (Ps. 2:4a). God will be amused by their plans to be rid of his control. When Domitian demands obeisance, keep the vision before you and, whatever the cost, be true to the eternal God of the universe.

Christians who are being persecuted because of their faith and those whose freedoms are being threatened need the comfort and encouragement of this vision. In April 1991 the Asia Press Service reported that in China the government had begun to impose restrictions because of the growing influence of the church and the growing numbers of Christians. House-church leaders had been arrested, and listening to foreign broadcasts was being tightly controlled. One province issued a decree that forbade believers to preach the gospel, hold house-church meetings, or mention the name of God outside the doors of government churches. In spite of the increased restrictions, believers were and still are willing to risk everything because of their love for Jesus Christ.

On a personal level, when discouragement, illness, problems, and unanswered "whys" confront us, we need to know that the God of the universe is in control and is interested in every detail of our lives. We need to learn to trust him, believing that he cares for us and that he has the answers. We need to learn to worship and praise him as the hosts of heaven do.

Have you learned to praise God in the midst of your burden and heartache? Try it! Praise lifts the burden. Praise shifts the focus of your attention away from yourself to God. Praise is the highest form of faith, for when you cannot see the answer and yet praise, you are telling God that you trust him, love him, and dare to leave the answer to him.

## THE WORLD'S DESTINY IS IN THE HANDS OF THE LAMB (REVELATION 5)

Revelation 4 and 5 form a unit; one vision encompasses both chapters. In chapter 4, the *throne* holds the center of attention. In chapter 5, the *Lamb* has the place of importance.

In the right hand of the Father is *the scroll*. This has been given several interpretations:

> [The scroll] represents God's eternal plan . . . it symbolizes God's purpose with respect to the entire universe throughout history and concerning all creatures in all ages and unto all eternity.[2]
>
> It is God's redemptive plan for the denouement of human history, the overthrow of evil, and the gathering of a redeemed people to enjoy the blessings of God's rule.[3]
>
> It is the book of the destinies of the world; it contains the record of that which is to happen in the last times; it is . . . the book of history written in advance.[4]
>
> The scroll is God's redemptive plan, foreshadowed in the Old Testament, by which he means to assert his sovereignty over a sinful world and so to achieve the purpose of creation.[5]

This vision tells us that God has a purpose for the world and that nothing can frustrate his purpose. God will carry out his will.

The scroll is completely sealed with seven seals, and, in order for God's purposes to be fulfilled, it must be opened. John weeps that no one in all the universe is worthy to open the scroll, but he is comforted when an elder points him to the One who is worthy. The descriptions of Christ (v. 5) as the Lion of the tribe of Judah and the Root of David are messianic references from the Old Testament. John looks toward the throne, perhaps expecting to see a lion—the symbol of strength and power. Instead he sees a lamb, the symbol of innocence and submission. The lamb appears as if it had been slain. Jesus' death gives him all power and authority, as symbolized by the seven horns. The number *seven* symbolizes completeness and perfection. The seven eyes symbolize intelligence and insight. Jesus is the all-seeing, the all-knowing One, possessing all power and authority.

The Lamb takes the scroll from the right hand of the Father, reminding us of these words in Rev. 1:1: "The revelation . . . which God *gave* him . . ." (italics added). The book of destiny is in the hands of the Lamb. Jesus is the only One who gives meaning to history. "In him all history will be consummated" (Eph. 1:10, *Phillips*). Unless a person believes and possesses the hope that Christ is coming again to end present history and usher in a glorious future for the church of God, then history will seem to have no goal and will seem meaningless.

Social and economic analysts, ecologists, and environmentalists are concerned about the future of our world. They are offering suggestions and solutions that need to be heard and implemented, but many of their solutions are based on naturalistic philosophies. Ultimately, only Christ has the real solution. He alone is worthy to open the scroll and to bring to fulfillment God's destiny for the world. His suffering and death makes him victorious and therefore worthy to open the seals of destiny.

When the Lamb takes the scroll (vv. 8-10), all heaven bursts into song. The living creatures and the elders lift their voices in praise to the Lamb. They hold bowls of incense, which represent the prayers of the saints. What a beautiful thought! When Christians pray on earth, their prayers are backed by all the hosts of heaven and affect the destiny of the world.

They sing a *new song*. The Revelation is a book of new things. A new thing will now take place as the Lamb breaks the seals of the scroll, thus bringing to completion God's purpose for his world. The song is new because Christ always brings a new quality to life.

In this scene, Jesus is crowned with glory and honor because of his suffering and death. He has paid with his blood in order to redeem all people—to set them free from the slavery of sin. To those who have accepted his offer, he has given all the rights of the kingdom; they are priests and rulers.

Now the circle of praise grows larger as another group of angels, numbering in the thousands of thousands, takes up the song of redemption. Soon the whole universe is filled with song to the One on the throne and to the Lamb. What a glorious service of worship!

## LEARN THE MEANING OF TRUE WORSHIP

All worship is to be directed toward God the Father and Jesus the Redeemer. Music and singing play an important part in worship. True worship honors God for who he is and for what he has done. The worship of heaven is joyful, exuberant, and beautiful, blended into perfect harmony by the fullness of the Holy Spirit. Ponder the lessons you have learned about worship from these heavenly scenes.

Lord, teach us to worship as the hosts of heaven do.

> Holy, holy, holy! Lord God Almighty!
> All thy works shall praise thy name in earth and sky and sea.
> Holy, holy, holy, merciful and mighty!
> God in three Persons, blessed Trinity!

Reginald Heber, 1783–1826

# Lesson 4

## God Keeps His Own Secure

### REVELATION 6–7

Review previous lessons by consulting the outline chart on page 14. Note that the first division of the book, Preparation (chapters 1–5), has now been completed. From the first five chapters, choose one idea or concept that tells how God encourages and prepares his people for the judgments to come.

Chapter 1:

Chapter 4:

Chapters 2–3:

Chapter 5:

Read chapters 6 and 7 and take note of what you see, hear, and feel. Recall that in the previous lesson, we saw the Lamb take from the hand of God the scroll of destiny that was sealed with seven seals. In chapter 6, six of the seals are opened, revealing a tragic picture of world history. Keep in mind that the scroll is in the hands of the Lamb.

#### Study Questions

REVELATION 6:
THE SEALS ARE OPENED—JUDGMENT BEGINS

1. Read Rev. 6:1-8 and note the symbolic description and symbolic meaning of the four horsemen of the apocalypse: Rider #1, Rider #2, Rider #3, Rider #4.
2. There are several opinions as to the identity of the first rider.
   a. What do you think he represents? (See pp. 54–55, Study Helps and Commentary.)
   b. What are the indications that he is active today?
3. Read Rev. 6:9-11. This scene, which shifts from earth to heaven, pictures the Christian martyrs.
   a. What do they ask? Why?

b. What do you think God's answer to them means?

4. The events related to the first five seals have always been and always will be a part of human history. What relevance, in your opinion, do the seals have to contemporary world conditions? Be as specific as you can.
5. Read Rev. 6:12-17, an apocalyptic description of the end time. While on earth, Jesus used similar descriptions. (See Mark 13:24-25.)
   a. Note seven areas of nature that are affected.
   b. List the seven classes of people, who represent all who have rejected Christ.
   c. What causes their fear? (vv. 16-17)
   d. A lamb is considered to be the most gentle, harmless animal. Yet here we read about the "wrath of the Lamb," also referred to by some as the "wrath of love." What is meant by this wrath of the Lamb? (v. 16)
   e. This scene pictures the terror and despair of those who have refused the claim of Christ on their lives. Now the full realization dawns on them. All that Christ has said is true, and now they must experience his rejection rather than his love. What a tragedy! Pause for a few moments to silently pray for those who have neglected or rejected Christ. Perhaps there is someone for whom you are especially concerned.

## REVELATION 7: GOD'S PEOPLE ARE SECURE

Six seals have been opened, and now we would expect to see the seventh seal opened and Christ to appear immediately. Instead, there is an interlude (chap. 7), the purpose of which is to encourage God's children before the next series of judgments is revealed.

1. Read Rev. 7:1-3. This vision, which John sees on earth, symbolizes God's perfect control. No destructive judgment (four winds) can come except by God's permission. Even in the midst of judgment, the people who are utterly devoted to God (servants) are secure (sealed).
2. Read Rev. 7:4-17. These verses give the symbolic picture of the church of Jesus Christ. The first group, the sealed followers of

the Lamb who live on earth, is the church militant (Rev. 7:4-8); the second group is the victorious saints in heaven, the church triumphant (Rev. 7:9-17).

a. What other interpretations of the 144,000 have you heard?

b. The important thing to consider here is the symbolic meaning of this vision. What encouragement would it bring to Christians who are experiencing persecutions and severe trials?

3. Reread Rev. 7:9-17. The group pictured here is too large to count. Only God knows the exact number of people who belong to him.

a. Which words does John use to symbolize the universality of the group? (v. 9) to symbolize victory?

b. For what do the multitudes praise God? (v. 10)

c. What seven qualities do the angels ascribe to God? (v. 12)

d. Some people may believe that because they have done heroic deeds for Christ—even suffered or died for him—that Christ will welcome them into heaven. What is the only thing that qualifies a person to be in heaven? (v. 14b) Explain the meaning of this verse in your own words.

e. What is your understanding of the great ordeal? (v. 14b)

f. What do you learn about heaven in verses 15-17?

g. What do you look forward to most as you contemplate heaven?

## SUMMARY THOUGHTS

Page through a hymnal and find hymns about heaven. Note the phrases and ideas that find their source in the Revelation. If you are studying with a group, share some of your favorites. Thank God that his loving eye is on you and that he will keep you secure in life and in death. Thank him for the reality of heaven and for all those who are now rejoicing before his throne.

## LESSON 4
## GOD'S PEOPLE ARE SECURE
## REVELATION 6–7

### Study Helps and Commentary

In the first chapters of the Revelation, readers are encouraged and strengthened by the visions of the risen, glorified Lord. They see him in the midst of his church, helping and healing. They listen as he examines the churches, and are encouraged to examine their own lives, to confess their shortcomings and sins, and to invite Christ to fill their lives with meaning. Only then can they be prepared to live and die for him should they be called to do so.

In Revelation 4 and 5, readers are permitted to look into heaven and see a scene that encourages their fainting hearts: God on the throne is being adored and worshiped by the whole company of heaven, and the Lamb is being praised by a universal chorus of worshipers because he alone is worthy to open the scroll. The scroll is about to be opened and the judgments will be revealed.

As the judgments are revealed, we must remember that the scroll and the judgments are in the hands of Christ. God is in control; he will keep his own people safe and secure.

## THE SEALS ARE OPENED—JUDGMENT BEGINS (REVELATION 6)

The drama on the stage of history is about to begin. The four living creatures summon the four horsemen who ride into the earth in rapid succession.

*The first rider* (Rev. 6:2) has been interpreted several different ways. Some interpreters believe he symbolizes Christ because he rides a white horse and wears a crown. Others believe he represents the word of God, which goes forth into the world to conquer. Another view is that he represents conquest.

Since the other three horsemen each represent a form of disaster on the earth, it would be logical to view this first horseman as representing an aspect of judgment. He rides forth as a "Christ figure" and looks very much like Christ as depicted in Rev. 19:11-12. His purpose is to appear as a would-be savior and thus to conquer people's minds with propaganda and promises. Millions of people throughout history—even in our own day—have been enslaved through this kind of bloodless conquest. This rider reminds us of the man of lawlessness, whom Paul describes as the one who "opposes and exalts himself above every so-called god or object of worship, so that he takes his seat in the temple of God, declaring himself to be God" (2 Thess. 2:4).

This rider is active today, perhaps as never before, intent on capturing the hearts and minds of people through empty promises and lies. A recent survey states that nearly twenty-five million North Americans have joined cults. Like the rider on the white horse, these cults appear benign and harmless. However, all false religions pose an ominous threat to the Christian community, for such groups cannot tolerate the claim of Jesus Christ that he is the way, the truth, and the life, and that no one comes to the Father but through him (John 14:6).

*The second rider* (Rev. 6:3-4) is astride the red horse of war. Note that "its rider was permitted to take peace from the earth." This does not mean that God approves of or sends war, but he uses it for his purposes. Here, war becomes a judgment.

*The third rider*, on a black horse (Rev. 6:5-6), carries a pair of scales used for weighing grain. A voice cries out, "A quart of wheat for a day's pay, and three quarts of barley for a day's pay, but do not damage the olive oil and the wine!" The condition described here refers not only to famine, but also to the fact that food is scarce and expensive.

*The fourth rider*, on the pale green horse (Rev. 6:7-8), symbolizes death. This death seems to be a result of the sword, famine, pestilence, and wild beasts. Hades, which is interpreted as the grave, underworld, or place of the dead, follows death perhaps to gather all those who have been killed by the plagues. But note that God limits his power. This rider is given power over only a fourth of the earth.

As we learn the symbolic meaning of each rider, we realize that they have always been a part of the human condition. Since the world began, dictators have tried to conquer people's minds with deception and lies. There have always been wars and bloodshed, often as a result of the conquest by the rider on the white horse. There have always been famine, scarcity, disease, and death as a result of the disasters represented by the first three horsemen. Jesus indicated that conditions would be even more severe toward the close of the age (Mark 13; Matt. 24). Hanns Lilje in *The Last Book of the Bible* says, "We understand that at the end of world history there will be an unparalleled conflict, which can only be endured by God's grace."[1]

*The fifth seal* reveals the martyrs' souls under the altar of God (Rev. 6:9-11). Just as animals in the Old Testament were slaughtered on the altar of sacrifice and their blood poured out at the base of the altar, so these Christians, through their martyrdom, are sacrifices to God. They have remained true to his Word and have witnessed fearlessly for Jesus. Since the life is in the blood (Lev. 17:11-14), their souls under the altar represent their lives poured out in martyrdom.

The souls under the altar cry out, "How long?" They plead for vindication of God's glory, for their martyrdom is really an attack on God himself. This is not a cry for personal vengeance, but a desire that righteousness might conquer evil and that the kingdom of God might come speedily. They appeal to God's sovereignty, holiness, and truth, for he has promised to vindicate his own. They pray that God will act and reveal his justice by ending the martyrdom of Christians. God answers by giving each of them a white robe, symbolic of the victory and blessedness of heaven. He tells them to rest until the number of the martyred is complete, until all are accounted for and no one is overlooked. This does not mean that God has a fixed number of people in mind who will be martyred. It indicates that the end is not yet here and that, throughout the history of the Christian church on earth, there will be martyrs and that God knows each one.

*The sixth seal* introduces a scene that is associated with the end of the world. The graphic descriptions of the convulsions in nature are borrowed from Old Testament references to the day of the Lord. (See Joel 2:31; 3:14-15; Isa. 13:9-10; and Hag. 2:6.) Jesus uses similar descriptions in Matt. 24:29 and Mark 13:24-25. Note that these disturbances touched all of nature and every class of people, from the highest to the lowest. However, the wicked are filled with terror, for they have rejected Christ. They try to hide from the wrath of the Lamb. "God's wrath is the wrath of love, which even in anger is out to save, to amend, and to redeem the one it loves."[2] His wrath is "the consuming passion of his holy love that wills to destroy all that is unloving and untrue."[3] God's wrath is the reaction of his holiness against sin.

God's wrath also shows that he cares about his own and will vindicate them. Wickedness—and all who reject Christ and persecute his children—will one day be judged. God has not forgotten his suffering children. The blood of the martyrs calls out to him, and he hears. They are comforted by the assurance that God will vindicate them in this time.

> "In no place in this section is John trying to terrify the saints. He is using familiar apocalyptic imagery to reassure them. God is bringing his purposes to pass, and he will do so though it means that this world order, and indeed this whole mighty universe, pass away."[4]

## GOD'S PEOPLE ARE SECURE (REVELATION 7)

The Lamb has opened the seals one by one, revealing judgments that increase in intensity and severity. At the end of the sixth seal, we might expect the final judgment and the coming of Christ to follow immediately, but other judgments must take place first. The events following the opening of the sixth seal are so horrendous that all people who have not acknowledged Christ as Savior and Lord, from kings to slaves, cry out, "Who is able to stand?"

Revelation 7 answers this question. There are those who *are* able to stand. They are God's own, his sealed ones. They are safe and secure in the midst of tribulation, for God has his eye on them and will not let them go. They may be martyred for his sake, but they will be safe and secure with him in heaven forever.

Thus, before the seventh seal is opened, an interlude describes those whom God has made secure. We see *four angels standing at the four corners of the earth*, one each at the extreme north, south, east, and west. They are ready to allow the winds of persecution and tribulation to blow their fury on the earth. But the four angels are restrained by another of God's angels, the one who bears the seal of God. God is still on the throne of the universe! A wind cannot blow, a calamity cannot touch the earth, unless God gives his permission. Jesus says that not one sparrow falls to the ground without the Father knowing it (Matt. 10:29). The chief reason God stays these storms of fury is for the servants of God, his children on the earth. Before the final storms of the seventh seal can be unleashed, God makes it clear to his children that, come what may, they are secure in him, for he has sealed them on their foreheads (Rev. 7:1-3).

What is meant by the sealing of the servants of God? A seal on any official document indicates authenticity, ownership, and protection. It is a mark that can be seen clearly, indicating to whomever is handling the document that it is to be respected and treated with care. God's seal on his children's foreheads cannot be seen. It is an inner, spiritual reality. It is God's Holy Spirit witnessing with our spirits that we are children of God. God sealed us in baptism, claiming us for his own. His word is filled with promises of care, safety, and protection for his children:

> I have called you by name, you are mine. . . . I will be with you. (Isa. 43:1-2)
>
> Do not fear, for I am with you, do not be afraid, for I am your God; I will strengthen you, I will help you, I will uphold you with my victorious right hand. (Isa. 41:10)
>
> For the mountains may depart and the hills be removed, but my steadfast love shall not depart from you. (Isa. 54:10)

These are but a few of God's wonderful promises to his children that assure us that we are sealed and belong to God. With Paul, we can joyfully affirm:

> I am convinced that neither death, nor life, . . . nor things present, nor things to come, nor power, . . . nor anything else in all creation, will be able to separate us from the love of God in Christ Jesus our Lord. (Rom. 8:38-39)

God's purpose in assuring his children that we have been sealed is to give us courage and hope when the fierce winds of calamity, persecution, and tribulation come upon the earth. Even in the midst of suffering, we can look up confidently to him and affirm, "I am his; God on the throne is my Lord. His promises are my security. He will keep me the whole way home."

The number *144,000* (Rev. 7:4-8) has been given several interpretations. One view states that the 144,000 represent Jews who have come to Christ through the preaching of the two witnesses (Revelation 11) during the reign of antichrist. However, as George Ladd points out, this passage (Rev. 7:4-8) does not refer to salvation, but to the sealing or protection of those who have already been saved.[5] Furthermore, we might ask why only Jews will be sealed or spared from martyrdom while a large number of Gentiles will be martyred.

A more common view holds that the 144,000 represent the church universal, the "spiritual Israel" made up of both Jews and Gentiles. The 144,000 are mentioned again in Rev. 14:3, where they are specifically referred to as those "who have been redeemed from the earth." The fact that only twelve thousand from each tribe are sealed may symbolize that only those who belonged to the "spiritual Israel," who are truly members of the body of Christ, can have security in the midst of persecution. Others may outwardly belong to Israel, the church, but only a personal relationship with Jesus Christ will keep them secure.

The number 144,000, as other numbers in the Revelation, must be interpreted symbolically. It is a multiple of ten (completeness) and twelve (the people of God). It means fullness and completeness and refers to the totality of the redeemed. God knows just how many redeemed people there are; therefore, he can use a specific number. He knows each one by name. He will bring them all safely home to his house some day; not one will be missing.

*A great multitude* that cannot be counted is described in Rev. 7:9-17. This group, and the 144,000 just described, are not two different groups. They are one company, seen from two different aspects. The 144,000 represent the church militant on earth. The second group is the church triumphant in heaven.

The vision of the redeemed in heaven (Rev. 7:9-17) is one of the most beautiful and glorious visions in this book. Jews and Gentiles are in this group, some of whom have suffered martyrdom. All are safe in their heavenly home because they have remained faithful to Jesus Christ. Their white robes symbolize the righteousness and festivity of heaven. The palm branches speak of the joy of their victory. They stand confidently in the presence of the Lamb because he has bought them with his blood and brought them safely home. What a contrast to the picture in chapter 6 of those who have rejected the Lamb!

The redeemed sing out joyfully and loudly the theme of their song, gratitude for their salvation. They are in heaven through no merit of their own, only through the grace and love of God through Christ. All the angels and other heavenly beings mentioned in chapters 4 and 5 take up the song. The angels have never experienced salvation because they have never sinned. They stand in awe at what God is able to do for a sinner—calling, overcoming rebellion, forgiving, cleansing, and purifying so that a sinner is able to stand in the very presence of Christ! Small wonder that the angels join in the liturgy of heaven with their sevenfold blessing (Rev. 7:12).

When one elder asks John the identity of the white-robed throng, he respectfully and graciously asks the elder to answer his own question. What a beautiful answer! The redeemed from every nation are in heaven because they have confessed their sins and accepted cleansing through the blood of Jesus. They have been faithful to Christ in the midst of the great ordeal through which they have passed.

What is meant by the great ordeal? (Rev. 7:14) One interpretation holds that it refers to all the trials, troubles, and persecutions through which Christians must pass in every age. Other interpretations say that the great tribulation (ordeal, NRSV) is a period of intense persecution and martyrdom of Christians that will occur before the end of the world. Mark 13:19 and Dan. 12:1 point to such a time of suffering.

Perhaps we can interpret the great ordeal as a combination of these two views. Throughout history, many of God's saints have come through great tribulation and are now before the throne of God. But toward the end of the age, as Scripture indicates, there will be a period of severe testing and persecution (Matt. 24).

Note the past tense: "*have come* out of the great ordeal" (italics added). Even though John looks at both the past and the future tribulation, he speaks as if it has already occurred. This tells us something about interpreting the Revelation. Time in this book is not chronological; events do not follow one another as dated by a calendar. In all the visions, John is free in his use of time as it relates to events and in his use of symbolism. Since the visions flow so freely, it is difficult to limit them to a specific time or place.

The true purpose of this beautiful vision of heaven is to encourage persecuted Christians. Regardless of their harassment and persecution by the non-Christian world, Christians who continue to be loyal to Christ, even if it means martyrdom, can know that a welcome awaits them in the Father's house. They will be in the very presence of Jesus, whom they have not seen and yet have loved; they will see him face to face and will serve him ceaselessly.

The redeemed will be sheltered by God on the throne (Rev. 7:15). The picture here is of God spreading a tent over his own to shelter them. The tense changes to the future, perhaps indicating that John is visualizing the condition of the redeemed in the new heaven and new earth. In God's presence, there will be perfect satisfaction and contentment, no more troubles, trials, or sorrows. The Lamb becomes the Shepherd, reminding us of the beauty of the Twenty-third Psalm. There will be no more crying, for God will wipe every tear from their eyes.

This vision is meant to give comfort, courage, and hope to suffering Christians. It says to them, "Remain faithful to Christ. Witness boldly for him regardless of the cost, for there is a great future in store for you. It will be worth it all when you see Christ."

O happy day when we shall stand
Amid the heavenly throng,
And sing with hosts from every land
The new celestial song,
The new celestial song.

Wilhelm Andreas Wexels, 1797–1866
Tr. George Alfred Taylor Rygh, 1860–1943

# Lesson 5

## The Prayers of Christians Move the Hand of God

### REVELATION 8–9

Consult the outline chart on page 14. Note that we are in the second division of the Revelation entitled "Judgment." In our last lesson, we studied the first series of judgments—the seals. Review the content of each seal.

In this lesson, we will study the second series of judgments—the trumpets. Many commentators believe that the three series of judgments depicted in the Revelation extend throughout history—that each series repeats the previous series but with added features. Other commentators believe that the seals relate to all of history and that the trumpets and bowls relate specifically to the end of the age.

Read Revelation 8 and 9 to gain a general idea of these chapters. Describe your impressions and reactions.

#### Study Questions

#### REV. 8:1-5: PREPARATION FOR THE TRUMPET JUDGMENTS

1. Read Rev. 8:1-2. Note that the seventh seal introduces the seven trumpets. Try to imagine yourself experiencing that half hour's silence. What effect would it have? What purpose would it serve?
2. What does Rev. 8:3-5 tell us about the importance and power of prayer?

#### REV. 8:6-13: THE FIRST FOUR TRUMPETS

1. Read Rev. 8:6-12. On a piece of paper, complete the following chart about each of the first four trumpets:

| | *What happens* | *At what directed* | *The results* |
|---|---|---|---|
| 1st | | | |
| 2nd | | | |
| 3rd | | | |
| 4th | | | |

2. What is the significance of the repetition of the phrase *a third of*?
3. Although these judgments are directed at the natural creation, how do they affect people? What effects of these judgments do you see today? (The figure of a trumpet, often an instrument of warning, is appropriate for what you see here.)
4. Read Rev. 8:13. According to the eagle's cry, at whom are the woes that follow directed? Who are these people?

## REV. 9:1-12: THE FIFTH TRUMPET

1. Read Rev. 9:1-12. Who opens the bottomless pit? What comes from the pit first? What follows?
2. What are the locusts not permitted to do?
   a. Who are the locusts permitted to torture (9:4b) for five months?
   b. How does Rev. 9:6 indicate the severity of their torture?
   c. Who leads this demonic horde? (9:11)
3. This whole scene seems to picture, in symbolic language, demonic forces that plague those who reject Christ. It may also refer to the terrible evil of which people are capable when they refuse to receive the power of the gospel into their lives and thus exist under the power of sin and Satan. What evidence of this kind of evil do you see in our world today?

## REV. 9:13-20: THE SIXTH TRUMPET

1. Read Rev. 9:13-19. In what respect is the sixth trumpet judgment more severe than the fifth? (Think in terms of the demonic animals in each judgment and what they are permitted to do to godless people.)
2. The golden altar (9:13) reminds us again that God's people and their prayers are very important to God. He hears their cries and answers them. Why is this reminder needed?

3. What does the symbolism of an exact time of judgment (9:15) tell us about God and his judgments?
4. How large is this demonic cavalry? (9:16) How large a part of the human race does this army kill? (9:18)
5. Which words does John use to describe the ferociousness, power, and demonic origin of the horses?
6. An encouraging note in these chapters is that God is in control and has greater power than Satan. But the rebellion of the human race makes it necessary for God to act. In each of the following verses, underline in your Bible the words indicating that evil can exert itself only in limited ways: Rev. 9:3, 4, 5, 15.

## REV. 9:20-21: THE CALL TO REPENTANCE

1. Read Rev. 9:20-21. What is the reaction of the godless world to the trumpet judgments?
2. Note the things that the godless people refuse to give up and for which they do not repent.
   a. Relate their rebellion to the present world scene.
   b. What indications do you see of God's judgments today on people who refuse to obey his laws?
3. According to these verses, what is God's purpose in permitting judgments to come upon this world? In what way do his judgments express his love and concern for his people and his creation?
4. Old Testament prophets often viewed natural disasters as judgments from God and a call to repentance. Do you believe that disasters cause people to turn to God today? Why or why not? What examples come to mind?

## A CALL TO PRAYER

Remember this encouraging thought: God will silence all the choirs of heaven to listen to your prayers. What prayer concerns come to your mind as you think through these chapters? Write a few short prayers. If you are studying with a group, share your prayers.

## LESSON 5
## THE PRAYERS OF CHRISTIANS MOVE THE HAND OF GOD
## REVELATION 8–9

### Study Helps and Commentary

Apocalyptic descriptions of the end of the age accompany the opening of the seventh seal, which introduces the trumpet judgments. The first four seals (Rev. 6:1-8) describe events that have always been a part of the human experience—conquest, war, famine, and death. The events following the blowing of the trumpets are much more serious in nature. Here we see cataclysmic events and demonic forces invading the world—all in preparation for the final consummation.

### PREPARATION FOR THE TRUMPET JUDGMENTS (REV. 8:1-5)

The seventh seal is unlike the other six, for when it is opened, no plague follows. Rather, there is silence in heaven for half an hour. All the music of heaven is quieted! Why does this prolonged silence occur?

Imagine that you are in an auditorium waiting for a famous violinist to begin her concert. The hall is buzzing with the chatter of concertgoers. Then the artist walks onto the stage and lifts her bow. The chattering stops as the people wait expectantly for the concert to start. Imagine that this silent expectation lasts for half an hour, and you will grasp the image of what is happening in this passage. The silence in heaven intensifies the expectation and dramatizes the seriousness of the judgments to follow.

Another interpretation of this silence is that God quiets all the music of heaven so that he can hear the prayers of his saints. The prayers of God's people, which are heard in heaven, move God in his governing of the world.

*The incense* mingled with the prayers (8:3-4) may refer to Christ's intercessions on behalf of his suffering, persecuted church. The merits of Jesus make our prayers acceptable to God. In this passage, as the prayers rise to God, the answer comes as fire from the altar, is thrown on the earth, accompanied by thunder, lightning, and an earthquake. This is reminiscent of the scene when the fifth seal was opened. The souls under the altar—the martyrs—cried out to God for vindication of his justice. God answers the prayers, not only those of the martyrs but also those of all his persecuted, suffering children, by sending the trumpet judgments.

## THE FIRST FOUR TRUMPETS (REV. 8:6-12)

The trumpet judgments are grouped into two series of four and three each, as were the seals. The first four trumpets usher in catastrophes that affect the natural creation, and the last three trumpet judgments affect humankind. The judgments following the opening of the seals were all natural, ordinary occurrences, but the trumpet judgments add supernatural elements. The first four trumpet judgments are similar to the plagues of Egypt. They are partial, affecting only a third of the creation. The purpose of these trumpet judgments is to warn and call people to repentance.

The first trumpet affects the earth and its vegetation; the second affects the sea and ships; the third pollutes the rivers and springs of drinking water; and the fourth trumpet affects the luminaries in the sky. If is difficult to analyze in detail the symbolism associated with these four judgments. Leon Morris says, "We must insist that difficulty in harmonizing details should never worry us in this book. John is painting pictures, not writing scientific prose."[1] Much of the symbolism is rooted in the Old Testament. Jeremiah, for instance, refers to wormwood as being symbolic of God's judgment on his people who had disobeyed him. "Therefore thus says the Lord of hosts, the God of Israel: 'I am feeding this people with wormwood, and giving them poisonous water to drink' " (Jer. 9:15). Some of the symbolism may refer to contemporary events of that day. Various commentaries relate the burning mountain that "was thrown into the sea" to the eruption of Mount Vesuvius.

Some present-day readers of the Revelation may see a connection with the trumpet judgments in the following account. An article in the *New York Times* (June 18, 1991) labeled a gigantic asteroid hurtling toward earth as "the doomsday rock." Scientists believe that eventually it will hit the earth, with catastrophic results. The task that confronts scientists now is to find a way to divert the "doomsday rock" so it will not collide with the earth. Some scientists label the asteroid account an "environmental scare" and do not take it seriously. Other scientists are concerned.

Perhaps it is best not to attempt to relate the trumpet judgments to specific events, but to realize that serious natural disasters have occurred throughout history and that even more severe ones will occur in the future. God would impress on all people that he speaks through every earthquake and flood, through every disaster, calling people to repent while there is still time. While this call goes out primarily to the unrepentant, it seems that the people of God also suffer during these disasters.

The ecologists of our day would perhaps see significance in the four trumpet judgments. The depletion of the ozone layer and pollution of air and water are some of the environmentalists' concerns. God gave his people dominion over his creation, over the works of his hands, and put everything under their feet (Ps. 8:5-8). This privilege involves responsible use of God's creation. But because of carelessness and greed, our water, air, and even food have become polluted. We have defied God's law regarding the stewardship of nature, so nature suffers and, as a consequence, humanity suffers. In contrast to those who misuse God's creation, there are those who go to the opposite extreme, seeing the earth as divine. They teach that the earth should be worshiped as a god, often referred to as Gaia. Balance and wisdom are needed as we confront these environmental issues. The four trumpet judgments may not have any bearing on the ecological problem per se, for they seem to be more severe and climactic than what we face today. Yet scientists who are concerned with the environment have forced the world to face the fact that disaster may overtake this planet unless we take steps to halt environmental deterioration.

### *The Cry of the Eagle (Rev. 8:13)*

The first four trumpets have been blown, and three more judgments will follow. The cry of the eagle in midheaven, where all can see it, seems to divide the trumpet judgments into two groups. The eagle proclaims three woes, indicating that the next three trumpet blasts will bring even more serious plagues. The first four were directed at nature and at people only indirectly. But the fifth and sixth trumpet judgments are directed specifically at those who reject Christ. The woes are aimed at "the inhabitants of the earth" (Rev. 8:13).

This expression refers to people who have made this world their home. They live for materialistic values, giving little or no thought to the eternal.

In contrast, the Christian can sing, "I'm a stranger and a pilgrim. This world is not my home." We do not become so imbedded in the tinsel of this world that we forget that our real home is in the Father's house. These woes fall on those who have refused God's call to repentance and faith. "Sealed" Christians will be spared from these plagues. (See Rev. 9:4 and 16:2.)

## THE FIFTH TRUMPET (REV. 9:1-12)

With the blowing of the fifth and sixth trumpets, a new element is added, that of the supernatural or demonic. A star, symbolic of an angelic being, is given a key to the bottomless pit and is permitted to open it. Out of this abyss, which is hell itself, pour billows of dark smoke that cloud the air and darken the sun. Then follow swarms of locusts that sting like scorpions. They are not permitted to harm any vegetation, only people who do not have the seal of God on their foreheads. They are permitted to torment only the ungodly, those who have refused allegiance to Jesus Christ. This torment is for a limited time, symbolized by the five months. The suffering from this plague is so severe that people seek death, but it eludes them.

Rev. 9:7-11 contains a more detailed description of these locusts. They look like horses arrayed for battle. (An old Arab saying states that the locust has a head like a horse, a breast like a lion, feet like a camel, a body like a serpent, and antennae like the hair of a maiden.[2]) The picture John portrays reminds us of the plague of locusts inflicted on the Egyptians (Exod. 10:12-15) and the invasion of locusts described by Joel (1:4-20; 2:3-11).

Only those who have lived through an invasion of locusts can realize the horror and suffering of such an experience. Millions of locusts march in rank across the land, eating every vestige of green vegetation in their path, stopping for nothing. They go over the tops of buildings and through open windows and doors. When they fly, their mass blocks the light of the sun; the whirring of their beating wings reminds John of the sound of chariots rushing into battle.

What does this symbolism mean? These are not ordinary locusts, for they come out of hell. They are not permitted to destroy the green vegetation, as do ordinary locusts, but only to afflict people. They also have a demonic leader whose name is Apollyon, which means "destroyer."

John is describing demonic beings and the torture, darkness, devastation, hopelessness, despair, and terror that the power of darkness can inflict on those who follow the god of this world. The description of the locusts in Rev. 9:7-11 symbolizes the deceitfulness of Satan. He promises victory (golden crowns) and power to those who follow him, but the torture and devastation that he inflicts is much more serious than any natural locust plague.

The fifth trumpet judgment certainly describes sin's power and destruction in every age. This judgment may also refer to demonic activity at the end of the age. The great upsurge today of interest in cults, psychic powers, Satan worship, and witchcraft comes to mind as we study this passage in the Revelation. Many other demons are loose in the world today: demons of violence, bloodshed, racism, drug abuse, alcoholism, immorality, pornography, perversion, and more. These all have their origin in the "bottomless pit" and are abroad in the world to torture humankind with their sting.

The eagle in Rev. 8:13 warned of three woes that were to follow. With the blowing of the fifth trumpet, the first of these woes is now past, according to Rev. 9:12. Two more will follow.

## THE SIXTH TRUMPET (REV. 9:13-19)

The sixth trumpet is similar to the fifth trumpet in that it also brings forth an invading army. The locusts of the fifth trumpet are not allowed to kill humankind, only to torture them. But, the army of the sixth trumpet, made up of demonic horses, is permitted to kill a third of humankind.

After the sixth angel blows his trumpet, John hears a voice from the golden altar. This is the same altar mentioned in Rev. 8:3; it is the altar of incense that symbolizes the cry of the saints for God's justice to be shown through the deliverance of his people and the final establishment of his kingdom on earth. God answers these cries in the blowing of the sixth trumpet. The prayers of God's people move him to bring judgment on their enemies.

The voice from the altar commands that the four angels who are bound at the river Euphrates be released. This river formed the eastern boundary of the land of Canaan, beyond which lived the enemies of Israel—the Assyrians and the Parthians. The four angels represent evil angels and may also be the leaders of the demonic horde. They are released at the word of God and only in his time (Rev. 9:15). The number of the cavalry is so large that it cannot be counted, but John hears the number, two hundred million. As with other numbers in the Revelation, the two hundred million should be taken symbolically. It represents the vastness of God's judgment on the godless civilization. God permitted one-third of the unrepentant people to be killed as a warning and a call to those still living.

The description of the horses—their heads like lions' heads; the fire, smoke, and sulfur coming out of their mouths; and their serpentlike tails—all serve to describe the terror of these fiendish, demonic monsters. Notice that the emphasis is on the horses, not on the riders. It is the horses that have the power to inflict death.

This whole scene pictures war. To the first-century Christians, the huge cavalry may have meant the Parthians, skilled horsemen who lived beyond the Euphrates and who constantly threatened to invade Roman territory. However, we cannot limit this scene only to the Parthian threat or to Babylonian or Assyrian invasions. Perhaps it refers to the hellishness of all wars. Specifically, however, it refers to the end of the age when God will send judgment on the godless civilization in a final effort to get them to repent before the last trumpet sounds.

## THE CALL TO REPENTANCE (REV. 9:20-21)

Rev. 9:20-21 indicates that God looked for a response of repentance from those who have survived the horrible trumpet judgments. Through the fifth and sixth trumpet judgments, God is giving the unrepentant a taste of the terrible judgments that will come.

Does the sixth judgment cause them to repent? Evidently not. They continue to cling to materialistic values (the works of their hands), to their idols (also the works of their hands), to demon worship (closely associated with idol worship), and to their murders, sorceries, fornication, and thefts. The word translated "sorceries" comes from the Greek word *pharmakeia*, from which we get the English word "pharmacy." The root meaning refers to the use of drugs, often in connection with witchcraft.

It would seem logical that those who did not die during this terrible plague would turn to God and, terrified by all they have seen, cry out for mercy. Instead, they harden their hearts even more. They have become so entrenched in their life-style that not even stark tragedy can shake them loose. These are not only the "in-the-gutter" sinners but also the cultured and the religious people—all who have not submitted their lives to the lordship of Jesus Christ.

## WHAT MESSAGE DO THESE CHAPTERS HAVE FOR US TODAY?

Let us take prayer seriously, remembering that God takes our prayers into account as he governs the world. Let us join our prayers with those of oppressed people throughout the world, asking God to right every wrong and bring justice to earth.

Let us thank God that he has heard the prayers of countless people around the world. Cultural and religious walls have crumbled, and many countries are experiencing new freedoms. For the first time in years, Christians in some countries are permitted to have Bibles, read them openly, and worship freely. Pray for these Christians, that they will have the right spiritual leadership to teach them. Because of the present accessibility of these countries, many false religions are entering, seeking to fill the vacuum caused by many years of deprivation of the Word. Pray that Satan will be hindered from deceiving these new Christians.

Let us pray for our own nation, that it will repent of its sin and become, in truth, a Christian nation. Pray that we will witness to the world that "in God we trust."

Let us guard against any enchantment with psychic phenomena, no matter how innocent they may appear. Let us warn our young people of these dangers. The devil is real; he may promise a new "high," but this will always end in an eternal "low."

Let us ask God to give us concern and compassion for people who do not know Christ personally. Just as Jesus wept over Jerusalem, may that same love motivate us to tell people about the beautiful life they may experience in Christ, now and the future glory that is in store for God's children. Many people are unaware of the judgment that will come on the unrepentant world.

O God of earth and altar,
Bow down and hear our cry;
Our earthly rulers falter,
Our people drift and die;
The walls of gold entomb us;
The swords of scorn divide.
Take not thy thunder from us,
But take away our pride.

From all that terror teaches,
From lies of tongue and pen,
From all the easy speeches
That comfort cruel men,
From sale and profanation
Of honor, and the sword,
From sleep, and from damnation,
Deliver us, good Lord!

Gilbert Keith Chesterton, 1874–1936

# Lesson 6

# The Word of God Will Triumph

## REVELATION 10–11

Consult the outline chart of the Revelation on page 14. Note that we are in the second division of the book entitled "Judgment." We now have studied two series of judgments, the seals and the trumpets. Look back over the previous chapters and note which scenes take place on earth and which take place in heaven.

Read Revelation 10 and 11, keeping in mind that these chapters symbolize the preaching of the word of God and its reception and rejection. What are your initial responses to these chapters?

### Study Questions

#### REV. 10:1-7: THE UNIVERSALITY OF THE WORD

1. Read Rev. 10:1-7. Which words indicate that the mighty angel is closely associated with Christ and comes from the very presence of God?
2. How would this vision of the mighty angel, who gives the whole world a message from God, encourage Christians who were often ridiculed because they had faith in God's word?
3. What happens when the angel calls out? (v. 3)
   a. What does John plan to do? (v. 4)
   b. What is he told to do?
4. The angel swears by God so the readers can be sure the oath will be fulfilled. How is God described in the oath? (v. 6)
   a. What is promised in the oath? (vv. 6-7)
   b. How would this description of God and the content of the oath encourage tested and tried Christians living in any age?

#### REV. 10:8-11: THE EFFECT OF THE WORD

1. Read Rev. 10:8-11. What is John commanded to do?
   a. What happens when he obeys the command?

b. What does this mean for John?
2. What lessons do verses 8-11 hold for anyone who wishes to bring God's word to others? What aspect of witnessing may be "bitter"? what "sweet"?

## REV. 11:1-13: THE WITNESS OF THE WORD

Chapter 11 is perhaps the most difficult chapter in the Revelation to understand. Biblical scholars do not agree on its interpretation, so do not become discouraged if you cannot understand all the details.

1. Read Rev. 11:1-13.
   a. What is John instructed to do? (v. 1) What is he instructed not to do? (v. 2)
   b. Of which two Old Testament leaders do the two witnesses described in Rev. 11:6 remind you? (See Exod. 7:17-21 and 1 Kings 17:1.)
   c. What happens to the witnesses when their task is done? Who is their enemy?
   d. What is the reaction of the hostile world to the death of the witnesses? (Rev. 11:9-10)
   e. How does God vindicate his witnesses? (Rev. 11:11-12)
   f. How does the world react to the signs that accompany the resurrection of the two witnesses? (v. 13)
2. If we believe that the two witnesses symbolize the church bringing the word of God to a hostile world, what might the following symbolic descriptions tell us about the preaching and witness of the church?
   Sackcloth (Rev. 11:3)
   Two olive trees, which produce oil—a symbol of the Holy Spirit—for the lamps (see Zech. 4:3-6)
   Two lampstands
3. Some organizations today are trying to silence the voice of the church and, if possible, remove every evidence of Christianity from public view and practice. Give some examples of this. What should we be doing to combat their influence?
4. Have you ever experienced any suffering or rejection because of your witness for Christ? If so, describe what happened.

REV. 11:14-19: THE TRIUMPH OF THE WORD

1. Read Rev. 11:14-19. As the seventh trumpet sounds, we would expect another plague to follow. Instead, John looks down the eons of time and sees the final triumph of Christ.
   a. Recall what followed the opening of the seventh seal (Rev. 8:1).
   b. In contrast, what occurs when the seventh trumpet is sounded? (Rev. 11:15)
   c. What is the theme of the heavenly chorus? (v. 15)
   d. For what do the elders thank and praise God? (vv. 16-18)
2. What encouragement would these verses bring to witnesses living in any age?

CONTEMPLATE YOUR TRIUMPH IN CHRIST

God calls us to be faithful witnesses, even though it may mean opposition, rejection, or even martyrdom. But God promises us a glorious victory if we remain faithful to him, a triumph that will far outweigh any suffering we may have to endure. Play a recording of the "Hallelujah Chorus," which was inspired by Rev. 11:15. As you listen, praise God for the triumph that Jesus Christ will bring to this world when he comes again. Thank him, too, that you will share his victory even now as you abide in him.

## LESSON 6
## THE WORD OF GOD WILL TRIUMPH
## REVELATION 10–11

### Study Helps and Commentary

It is interesting to note how the scenes in the Revelation shift back and forth from earth to heaven. This indicates how fluid apocalyptic literature is. Because John is in the spirit as he sees visions from God, he is not bound by time or space.

In the first three chapters, John is introduced to his first vision. On earth, he sees the glorified Christ and hears his messages to the seven churches. In chapters 4 and 5, the scene shifts to heaven. John views and hears the worship of heaven, the center of which is

God on the throne and the Lamb holding the scroll, which symbolizes God's redemptive purpose in history. In chapter 6, the scene shifts again to earth as the seals are opened and judgment begins. In the interlude in chapter 7, the scene is again in heaven, followed by a return to earth for the more severe judgments in chapters 8 and 9. Following the trumpet judgments, another interlude (Rev. 10–15) begins on earth and shifts to heaven for more songs of the martyrs.

Consult the outline chart on page 14 and notice that before each judgment occurs it seems as if the curtain of heaven is pulled aside so that readers may look into heaven and see its beauties and hear its glorious music. The purpose of these glimpses of heaven is to assure Christians that God and the lamb are in control (the martyrs are singing songs of victory). These images of heaven encourage and strengthen those being persecuted so that they will remain faithful to God no matter how severe the testing, knowing that their heavenly Father will care for them and bring them home someday.

## THE UNIVERSALITY OF THE WORD (REV. 10:1-7)

A dazzling vision is revealed to John. He sees an angel coming down from heaven. The angel is so huge that he is able to straddle the whole universe. His legs are like pillars of fire, his face shines like the sun, and he is enveloped in a cloud. The light of his face, shining through the cloud, forms a rainbow over his head.

The angel's appearance is much like that of Christ, and some interpreters say that he is Christ. But Christ is never called an angel in the Revelation, so this is an angel who is closely associated with Christ and who has come from the presence of God with a message for the whole world. In his hands the angel holds a little scroll, different from the one given to the Lamb in Revelation 5. The Greek word for "little scroll" may be translated "pamphlet." Because it is small, the scroll may be a limited revelation. But the scroll is open, indicating that the message is to be revealed to the whole world. When the angel speaks, his voice sounds "like a lion roaring," which indicates that it is loud enough for all to hear and that it manifests authority.

John must have understood what was said, for he was about to write the message down when he was hindered from doing so. Many people have speculated about the content of the seven thunders.

The fact that the message was to be sealed and not written down seems to indicate that only God has the answers to some mysteries. Although we cannot be sure what the angel said, thunder in Revelation is usually associated with judgment. The angel then swears by God himself that "there will be no more delay." This promise may indicate that the message refers to the final series of judgments, the bowls of wrath, which will begin when the seventh trumpet sounds. This promise also answers the cries of those under the altar (Rev. 6:9-10) and the prayers of the saints (Rev. 8:4), assuring them that God has not forgotten the injustices they have suffered. He assures them that he will soon vindicate them fully.

This whole scene encourages Christians to persevere in faith when fiery trials come. When we are tempted to give up, let us remember that although our suffering may seem to last an eternity, it will soon be over. "There will be no more delay." God will pour out his wrath on his enemies. His people will be vindicated and will reign with him in the new heaven and the new earth.

## THE EFFECT OF THE WORD (REV. 10:8-11)

John is commanded to eat the scroll. It is sweet in his mouth but bitter in his stomach. It is necessary that, as a true prophet of God, he assimilate and digest the whole word of God and experience both its bitter and sweet aspects. Only then could he proclaim to others its message in all its truth and power. This principle is true for every preacher and teacher of the word.

If the message in the little scroll contained the announcement of the final judgments, then the bitter part would be the responsibility of proclaiming the judgment of God's wrath on all who reject Christ and the pain of seeing many spurn this message. The sweet aspect would be proclaiming God's grace in Christ and the joy of seeing people respond to this message and thus be saved from the wrath to come.

Many interpreters believe that the angel and the little scroll refer to the worldwide proclamation of God's word by preachers and teachers throughout the entire gospel age. Preachers and teachers have the responsibility of presenting both the law and the gospel, of warning people about God's hatred of sin and their need for repentance, of presenting the way of salvation so clearly that none will doubt the way. Such preaching may cause some bitter reactions. There are some, for example, who do not want to hear about sin and God's judgment on the impenitent. Thus, preachers may be tempted to soften their message to make it more palatable. But if they have digested the whole word of God, they have a divine imperative to speak out fearlessly in love. Presenting the gospel of the love of Christ and seeing people respond to this gospel and grow in the grace and knowledge of Christ is sweet indeed.

In our personal experiences in the word, we also taste the bitter and the sweet. When we digest the word and it begins to show us our sin—weaknesses, failures, and disobediences—when we realize that we must die to self and let Christ be the absolute Lord of our lives, then we, too, may experience sorrow and bitterness. But if we acknowledge all that God shows us, accept his forgiveness, and grow in our surrender to his lordship, then we will experience the sweetness that the awareness of his presence brings.

## THE WITNESS OF THE WORD (REV. 11:1-13)

Rev. 11:1-13 has been given a variety of interpretations. We will look at two that are the most widely accepted.

*Some interpret this chapter literally.* They believe that the measuring of the temple (Rev. 11:1-2) refers to the actual rebuilding of the Jewish temple in Jerusalem toward the end of the age. The altar and the inner sanctuary, then, refer to Jews who believe in Christ. The outer court that is given over to the nations to be trampled on for forty-two months (or three-and-a-half years) refers to the great persecutions that the Jews will suffer during the reign of the antichrist. An explanation of *antichrist* is found on p. 90–91.

During this time, God will send two men, perhaps Moses and Elijah or two who come in their spirit. They will be filled with the Holy Spirit and given power to perform miracles. They will preach for three-and-a-half years and, as a result of their witness, many Jews will be won to Christ.

Some who believe this interpretation say that the 144,000 mentioned in chapter 7 are the Jews won to Christ during this period. These converted Jews will become missionaries to the whole world. After three-and-a-half years of preaching, the two witnesses will be killed by the antichrist, who is angered by their preaching. Their bodies will be left lying in the street, but after three-and-a-half days they will be resurrected and taken up to heaven. As a result of the events that follow their restoration and ascension, many people will come to faith. Most premillennialists hold this view.

*A more common view interprets this passage symbolically.* The temple represents the people of God. (Paul speaks of the temple of God as being made up of living stones and of each Christian as being a temple for the Holy Spirit.) The measuring is symbolic of protection and security and has much the same meaning as the sealing in chapter 7. The inner court refers to true Christians, in whose hearts the Holy Spirit dwells. They may suffer physically, yet they are protected and will be eternally safe. The outer court symbolizes those who are nominal Christians, who have accepted the outward forms of religion but lack inner spiritual reality. The nominal Christians are actually a part of the world, have adopted its way of thinking, and feel perfectly at home in the non-Christian world.

The forty-two months (or three-and-a-half years) symbolizes the entire gospel age, from the first coming of Christ to his second coming in glory. The two witnesses represent the witness of the true church and all its missionary activity. The witnesses are dressed in sackcloth because they preach repentance. They are so filled with the Holy Spirit that their words come forth with the power of fire as they proclaim God's wrath against sin. But the hostile world, symbolized by Jerusalem (which also rejected and killed the Messiah), rejects the message of the church. Toward the end of the age, the hostile world is inspired by Satan and finally silences the voice of the church. It loses its power and influence and is actually dead. When Christ comes again, however, it will be raised to life and caught up to be with him. Then the church's true glory and power will be manifested to the world. The sight will cause the world to be struck with terror and amazement, but it will not repent. An earthquake and other awesome signs will then precede the final judgment.

There are various additional symbolic interpretations of this chapter. Some people, for example, believe that two actual witnesses will appear toward the end of the age and will preach in the spirit of Moses and Elijah. The Jews of the Old Testament looked for a special messenger to come from God before the end of the age. Malachi identifies one of the messengers as Elijah (Mal. 4:5).

According to Hanns Lilje, in *The Last Book of the Bible*, "Jerusalem" is not to be taken merely symbolically. He says, "In some way or other the earthly, geo-historical Jerusalem will have its place in the history of the last days . . . that which God once willed for historical Israel and for Jerusalem will be fulfilled."[1]

Since most interpreters consider Revelation 11 to be the most difficult chapter in the book, and since most commentators do not agree on the interpretation of many of its details, we should humbly admit that we do not have the answers. However, we want to keep open minds and explore the possible answers. In our day, when thousands of Jews, especially from the former Soviet Union, are returning to Israel, we cannot write their return off as insignificant. Instead, we will ask, "Does their return have meaning in relation to God's program for the Jews?" When we realize that Jerusalem, which has been conquered about forty times during the centuries, is once again united under Jewish control, we will ask the same question. There are mysteries here to which only God knows the answers. Let us leave them with him.

Verse 14 states that the "second woe" has passed. This evidently refers to the judgments that follow the sixth trumpet. The first woe was the fifth trumpet judgment, according to Rev. 9:12. The third woe, which will soon come, refers to the final series of judgments, the bowls of wrath (Rev. 16).

## THE TRIUMPH OF THE WORD (REV. 11:14-19)

The scene now shifts to heaven, and John hears the heavenly choirs sing in exaltation because Christ has defeated every enemy and established the kingdom of God on earth. Christ is now the sovereign Lord.

We are reminded of the first strains of the "Hallelujah Chorus" in these words: "The kingdom of the world has become the kingdom of our Lord and of his Messiah, and he will reign forever and ever." The elders sing this song in anticipation of Christ's victory at his second coming. The remainder of the "Hallelujah Chorus" appears in Revelation 19.

In Rev. 1:8, God says that he is the Alpha and the Omega, the One "who is and who was and who is to come." In Rev. 11:17, the phrase *who is to come* is omitted, for in this anticipatory vision

Christ has already come and begun to reign. John, in his vision, looks into the future and sees these events as if they have already taken place. He also sees the final rage of the godless world and the final judgment (Rev. 11:18).

Another encouraging aspect of this vision is the open temple of God in heaven (Rev. 11:19), which reveals the ark of the covenant. The ark was kept in the Holy of Holies in the tabernacle and was seen only once a year by the high priest. It symbolized God's presence with his people and his mercy. The cover of the ark was called the mercy seat.

In this vision, the ark of the covenant is revealed for all people to see. No longer is God hidden. When Christ comes again, "He will dwell with them as their God; they will be his peoples, and God himself will be with them" (Rev. 21:3). His people "will see his face" (Rev. 22:4). Although the ark will bring comfort and the certainty of God's presence for his own, it will bring judgment, terror, and exclusion from his presence to the ungodly. This is symbolized by the lightning, loud noises, thunder, earthquake, and hail.

This vision brings much courage and hope to persecuted Christians. It motivates them to keep on witnessing fearlessly, with the certainty that the word of God is powerful and will accomplish all that God intends. Should their witnessing result in martyrdom, let them listen to the choirs of heaven who sing the words of the "Hallelujah Chorus," proclaiming Christ's victory, and their victory in him.

## WHAT MESSAGES DO THESE CHAPTERS HAVE FOR US TODAY?

Our greatest responsibility today is to be faithful witnesses, spreading God's powerful word to an often unheeding world. We must assimilate the word thoroughly. We must be filled and controlled by the Holy Spirit so that our words will have power. We must be true to the word of God, witnessing with boldness, knowing that we may experience misunderstanding, rejection, or suffering. Lilje says: It is more important to be a witness to Christ, as he himself was "*the* witness" absolutely, than to penetrate into the mysteries of the last days. . . . There is no other way to bear witness and to stand up for Christ before the world, than to bear it "openly," that is, by suffering. The true follower of Christ cannot evade the way of suffering.[2]

Writing in the *Chicago Tribune* (July 1992), Michael Hirsley mentions two trends that are definitely at odds with one another: first, the nation's fastest-growing churches are evangelical Christian; and, second, the nation's most widely accepted prejudice is anti-Christian. Hirsley concludes that these two counteracting forces appear destined to prosper through the 1990s. He also quotes Russell Chandler, former religion editor of the *Los Angeles Times* and author of *Racing Toward 2001*. In an interview, Chandler said, "Human beings are incurably religious. . . . Everyone is looking for transcendence, something beyond themselves. My point is they are looking for God."[3] In view of Hirsley's comments, we see that the church must continue to proclaim the gospel in the power of the Holy Spirit until people find God in the person of Jesus Christ. And this must continue in the face of opposition, ridicule, and criticism knowing that God's word is the power of God for salvation.

When we are tempted to be dismayed because of seemingly hopeless world situations, the vision that John saw should encourage us. We should listen often to the "Hallelujah Chorus" and keep the victorious song of the heavenly hosts in our hearts. Someday the kingdom of this world will become the kingdom of our Lord and of his Christ, and he will reign forever and ever. Hallelujah!

Jesus has delayed his second coming for many centuries. However, the words that John heard, "that there should be no more delay" (Rev. 10:6b), are more true today than ever before. As we live in the joyful expectation of his coming, this truth will give us a great sense of urgency as we go about the King's business.

Your kingdom come! O Father, hear our prayer;
Shine through the clouds that threaten everywhere;
Light from above, our only life and joy,
Show us the hope that nothing can destroy.

Your kingdom come; come too, God's glorious Son!
Oh, may our task for you be nobly done!
Faithful let all your servants be, and true,
Until they bring all nations home to you.

Margaret Rebecca Seebach, 1875–1948

# Lesson 7

## The Devil Is a Defeated Foe

### REVELATION 12–13

Glance at the outline chart of the Revelation on page 14 to see the progress of the book thus far. Now read chapters 12 and 13 and note your general impressions. Note the relation of chapters 12 and 13 to the other chapters in the second division of the book, Judgment. These two chapters explain the underlying cause of the conflict. They also bring strong encouragement to suffering Christians by assuring them that although it may seem as if the devil is winning the battle, he has been completely defeated by Jesus' victory at Calvary.

#### Study Questions

REV. 12:1-6: THE BIRTH OF THE CHILD—THE FOCUS OF THE CONFLICT

1. Read Rev. 12:1-6. Summarize the content of John's vision and note these details:
   the four characters in this drama
   the evil aim of the dragon
   God's victory over the dragon (vv. 5-6)
2. What do you think this symbolic vision means?
3. List instances in the life of Jesus when Satan tried to destroy him. (See Matt. 2:13-15; 4:5-7; Mark 11:18.)

REV. 12:7-12: THE DEFEAT OF THE ENEMY

1. Read Rev. 12:7-12. Between whom does the war in heaven take place?
   a. Note the names given to the devil.
   b. Which two words describe the means the devil uses? (vv. 9-10)

2. How is Satan's defeat described? (vv. 8-9) What causes the great celebration in heaven? (vv. 10-11, 12a)
3. What effect does Satan's defeat have on him? (v. 12b)
4. What are some ways in which the devil tried to deceive and accuse the early Christians? (See Acts 4:1-3; 7:54-58; 1 Peter 4:12, 14, 16, 19.) What encouragement would Rev. 12:11 bring to the early Christians?
5. In what ways is the devil showing his wrath and increasing his activity in our day? Be as specific as you can.
6. How does the enemy try to accuse and deceive you?
7. According to Rev. 12:11, what is the threefold way of gaining victory over the devil?
8. Do you think it makes any difference whether we regard the devil as a personality or merely as an evil in general? Why or why not?

## REV. 12:13-18: THE CONFLICT CONTINUES

1. Read Rev. 12:13-18. When the devil is not able to destroy the Messiah, on whom does he pour his hatred? (vv. 13, 17)
2. What symbolizes his attack on God's children? (vv. 15, 17)
3. What symbolizes God's protection of his children? (vv. 14, 16)

## REV. 13:1-10: THE BEAST FROM THE SEA

1. Read Rev. 13:1-10. Which statements about this beast indicate its close association with the dragon? (Compare 13:1 and 12:3.) Where does the beast obtain its power and authority? (See 13:2b, 4.)
2. How does the beast try to imitate Christ? (13:3)
3. What word (repeated four times in verses 1, 5, and 6) describes the beast's contempt of God? Give examples of how God is held in contempt and openly blasphemed in our society today.
4. Underline in your Bible the words in verses 5-7 indicating that God limits the beast's power and influence.
5. Whom might the beast have symbolized to the first-century Christians? (See p. 7 of the Introduction.)
6. Note that in 13:8 the verb tense changes to the future "will worship," perhaps indicating that this beast will not be limited

to just the first century. Which other "beasts" and their systems have been enemies of Christians and the church throughout history?

7. Who will worship this beast? (13:8) What will worship of the beast mean for Christians? (13:9-10)

## REV. 13:11-18: THE BEAST FROM THE EARTH

1. Read Rev. 13:11-18. The second beast does not appear to be as ferocious as the first beast, but wherein lies the subtle danger? (13:11)
2. What is the aim of the second beast? (v. 12) How does it go about accomplishing its goal? (vv. 13-15)
3. The beast is able to deceive "the inhabitants of earth" (v. 14), an expression used in the Revelation to describe the non-Christian world. What is the fate of those who refuse to worship the beast? (v. 15)
4. How does the second beast enforce the worship of the first beast? (vv. 16-17) What is the result of this on those who will not worship the beast?
5. The number *six* is the symbolic number for incompleteness and evil. Thomas Torrance, in his book on the Revelation, *The Apocalypse Today*, says, "666 is the number of every attempt to organize the world in a form that appears marvelously Christian but is in reality anti-Christian."[1] Think of one or two contemporary examples that illustrate this statement.
6. The second beast is also called the false prophet (16:13; 19:20). Many new religions are on the scene today. What questions should we ask to determine whether a religion is truly Christian? Base your questions on the statements of faith found in the Apostles' Creed and Nicene Creed. (Look in your hymnbook or service book for these creeds.)

## ENCOURAGEMENT FOR TESTED CHRISTIANS

These chapters impress on us the reality of Satan and his work throughout history. Christians know how subtle his attacks can be. Yet every Christian should know assuredly that the devil was defeated—stripped of his power—when Christ died on the cross and rose again. As Christian warriors, we must use that cross as a sword against Satan, reminding him that the blood of the Lamb has defeated him.

## LESSON 7
## THE DEVIL IS A DEFEATED FOE
## REVELATION 12–13

### Study Helps and Commentary

Two series of judgments have passed, the seals and the trumpets. The seventh trumpet has been blown, and two woes have been revealed. A third woe will come when the final judgments—the bowls of wrath—are poured out (Rev. 16). But before this happens, we meet the enemy who is behind all the opposition and persecution of Christians.

We have already seen the surface conflict between the world and the church. In chapters 12 and 13, we see the subsurface conflict, the war that is raging between Christ and Satan. We see that Satan has representatives on earth who do his fiendish work, and we are encouraged to know that the evil one has been dealt the death blow. Therefore, victory over him is available to every Christian.

### THE BIRTH OF THE CHILD—THE FOCUS OF CONFLICT (REV. 12:1-6)

As you read the above heading, you may have thought, Didn't the conflict with Satan begin before Christ was born? Yes, we saw it in the Garden of Eden (Gen. 3:15), where God spoke to the serpent about the enmity between him and the seed of the woman and predicted the fatal blow to the devil. Satan tried to hinder the birth of Christ, and it is this fact—his hatred of the Messiah—that this scene portrays. Although Rev. 12:1-6 brings to mind the birth of Jesus in Bethlehem, we must remember that it is a vision John sees in the heavens. Thus John goes beyond the historical birth of the Messiah; each figure is symbolic.

The woman represents the ideal people of God, the church. She symbolizes not only the Old Testament people of God, the true Israel that brought forth the Messiah, but also the New Testament people of God, the church (Rev. 12:17). Her glorious description (Rev. 12:1) reveals the beauty and honor that God has given to his people.

There is no doubt as to the identity of the dragon. It is the serpent of Genesis, Satan. Paul speaks of Satan as being the "god of this world" (2 Cor. 4:4). He is pictured here as a fierce monster. His seven heads, ten horns, and seven diadems or crowns depict his great might and universal power. The dragon's red color may symbolize that he is a murderer, a destroyer. The devil, who aims to destroy the Messiah, waits for the woman to give birth. Defeated in his attempt to kill the child, he pursues the woman who is preserved and protected by God.

The male child is Jesus the Messiah. John identifies him with the One mentioned in Psalm 2, the messianic psalm, who "is to rule all the nations with a rod of iron" (Rev. 12:5). As in other references to Christ in the Revelation, John is not interested in portraying the earthly life of Jesus. Rather, he portrays Jesus glorified in power and majesty. Hence, in this scene, the child is caught up to the throne of God, symbolizing Jesus' complete victory over Satan. The "snatching away" symbolizes Jesus' death and resurrection and his kingship with God the Father.

## THE DEFEAT OF THE ENEMY (REV. 12:7-12)

The war in heaven described in Rev. 12:7-12 is not to be taken literally. In symbolic language, John is telling us that Satan has been defeated. Jesus' death on the cross broke the power of Satan. Some commentators relate this incident to the fall of Satan described by the words of Isaiah: "How you are fallen from heaven, O Day Star, son of Dawn!" (Isa. 14:12). But here, as in the first paragraph, John goes beyond any point in time. He affirms that the devil has lost his place of power forever. John does not describe in detail how the defeat took place. Rather, he wants every tempted and tried child of God to know that the enemy has been dealt a death blow.

### *Character and Activity of Satan (Rev. 12:9-12)*

The name *Satan* means "the adversary." He is against God and Christ, against all that is holy and good. He is the enemy of every

Christian. In John 8:44, Jesus says of him, "He . . . does not stand in the truth, because there is no truth in him. When he lies, he speaks according to his own nature, for he is a liar and the father of lies." Notice the scope of Satan's influence; he deceives the whole world (Rev. 12:9).

Ponder the countless ways by which Satan is deceiving the world today: false religions that deny the deity of Christ, the fact of sin, and the need of a Savior and the cross; godless rulers who attempt to stamp out Christianity; Satan worship and the great upsurge of interest in the occult; the propaganda of the world; the false glamour of the materialistic way of life; and the big deception about the devil himself—that he does not exist and that anyone who believes he does belongs in the Dark Ages.

Satan is also described as being "the accuser of our comrades." He not only accuses Christians when they fall into sin, but also he emphasizes their guilt, causing them to focus on their sins rather than looking to Christ and accepting his forgiveness. Or, Satan accuses Christians falsely and makes them feel guilty for no reason. But he was defeated when Christ died on the cross and rose again. Therefore, a voice breaks out from heaven, celebrating this victory. The martyrs defeated Satan when they refused his temptations to deny Christ. They held faithfully to their word of testimony, counting faithfulness to Christ more important than life itself.

Rev. 12:12b seems to refer to the end of the age, when Satan, knowing he has little time left, will double his efforts to deceive and capture the minds of humankind.

## THE CONFLICT CONTINUES (REV. 12:13-18)

The devil's initial attack is against the child. But, when he realizes that, in spite of all his efforts to the contrary, Christ came to earth, died for the sins of the world, was raised in triumph, and ascended to the Father to rule victoriously, he turns his anger on the woman, who symbolizes the people of God. But God protects the woman by giving her the wings of an eagle, which symbolize preservation, support, and care.

Remember that in Exod. 19:4 God said to his people, Israel, through his servant, Moses, "You have seen what I did to the Egyptians, and how I bore you on eagles' wings and brought you to myself." The persecution of the Israelites in Egypt under pharaoh, God's awareness of their suffering, and his loving deliverance of his children out of the hands of pharaoh foreshadow the experience of Christians in this world. Christians live in hostile territory, and the devil pursues and persecutes them through other pharaohs, whether they be Neros, Domitians, or contemporary tyrants. But God is aware of his children's need and delivers them (Rev. 12:14). When the evil one spews out waters of hatred to engulf the woman, God gives her a way to escape and a place of security and safety.

When Satan is frustrated in his attempts to destroy the woman, he directs his attacks against individual Christians, "those who keep the commandments of God and hold the testimony of Jesus" (Rev. 12:17). This verse may refer to the final, great persecution toward the end of the age, when Satan, knowing that his time is short, intensifies his efforts to destroy Christians. Finally, the last verse of chapter 12 pictures the dragon standing on the shore of the sea, looking at the first beast rising out of the sea.

## THE BEAST FROM THE SEA (REV. 13:1-10)

The devil does his work on earth through his agents, who are devoted to doing his will. Rev. 13:1-10 introduces the first of these, the beast "out of the sea." The second beast "out of the earth" (Rev. 13:11-18) is also called "the false prophet" (Rev. 19:20) who enforces the edicts of the first beast.

John sees a horrible beast emerge from the sea. This beast is similar to the dragon (Rev. 12:3), for it also has seven heads and ten horns. John sees its body, fierce as a leopard, ready to leap on its prey. Its feet are like bear's feet, able to claw, tear, and destroy. Its mouth reminds us of Peter's description of the devil who prowls around "like a roaring lion . . . looking for someone to devour" (1 Peter 5:8).

The sea from which the beast rises is said to refer to people or nations. Isa. 17:12 reads, "Ah, the thunder of many peoples, they thunder like the thundering of the sea! Ah, the roar of nations, they roar like the roaring of mighty waters!" The blasphemous names on the beast's heads are often understood to refer to the blasphemy of Roman emperors who claimed divinity and demanded to be called "Lord," as did Domitian. Thus, this beast symbolizes any ruler or nation that usurps God's place. From the Babylonians, the Assyrians, the Roman Empire, down to the godless leaders and nations of our present day, all those who usurp God's place typify the first beast. The nations are symbolized by the seven heads and the kings by the ten horns.

*Possible Meanings of the Term* Antichrist

Some interpreters identify the beast that emerged from the sea with *antichrist.* This term is never used in the Revelation, but because it is commonly associated with this beast, we will consider the following interpretations.

Some believe that antichrist refers to the spirit of an age that is anti-Christian or anti-God. Others believe that the term refers to anything that would usurp the place of Christ in the life of a Christian. Another interpretation holds that antichrist refers to any teaching that obscures or distorts the gospel.

These interpretations describe the spirit of antichrist. However, some people believe that the spirit of antichrist will become incarnated in a person who will appear toward the close of the age. This view stresses the idea that antichrist will be embodied in a person rather than being only a spirit or an influence.

Only John, in his letters, uses the term *antichrist* in Scripture. He writes in 1 John 2:18, 22, "Children, it is the last hour! As you have heard that antichrist is coming, so now many antichrists have come. . . . Who is the liar but the one who denies that Jesus is the Christ? This is the antichrist, the one who denies the Father and the Son." In 1 John 4:3, John also refers to the spirit of antichrist as "every spirit that does not confess Jesus." Thus, it would seem that John uses the term *antichrist* to refer to incorrect doctrine concerning Christ as well as to individuals who propagate false teachings.

Some interpreters believe that Paul is referring to antichrist in the following passage:

> That day will not come unless the rebellion comes first and the lawless one is revealed, the one destined for destruction. He opposes and exalts himself above every so-called god or object of worship, so that he takes his seat in the temple of God, declaring himself to be God. . . . The coming of the lawless one is apparent in the working of Satan, who uses all power,

> signs, lying wonders, and every kind of wicked deception for those who are perishing, because they refused to love the truth and so be saved. For this reason God sends them a powerful delusion, leading them to believe what is false, so that all who have not believed the truth but took pleasure in unrighteousness will be condemned. (2 Thess. 2:3-4, 9-12)

Jesus also spoke of future false Christs and of the "desolating sacrilege" that would pollute the temple (Matt. 24:15) and perpetuate a severe persecution of Christians. Hanns Lilje says:

> In every respect the beast seems to be a caricature of the Messiah . . . as a caricature of Christ he is Antichrist. . . . The beast from the abyss, the symbol of Antichrist, is the most pictorial expression of the truth that the course of history is handed over to this power which fights against God, and that this anti-Christian power will not be overcome within the course of history, but that it will continue to grow, till at the very end of history it will be defeated, and completely annihilated by Christ, to whom all power alone belongs.[2]

*The Reign of the Beast*

The beast receives its power and authority from Satan (Rev. 13:2) and uses this devil-inspired pride to blaspheme God and deify itself (Rev. 13:5-6). The beast is so convincing that the whole godless civilization worships it (Rev. 13:7-8). It makes a last attack on Christians, the worst part being its demand for worship (Rev. 13:8). Christians, however, refuse to worship the beast, and for this they meet a martyr's death. Thus, the beast seems to conquer them (Rev. 13:7).

But John reminds us that the death of the martyr is in reality a crowning victory. God knows each martyr by name, and that name has been written in the book of life (Rev. 13:8). The martyrs have held to the faith of the crucified Lamb of God and so are safe and secure in the Father's house forever. John also reminds us that God is in control and that the beast would have no power unless permitted by God. Therefore, whether we are taken captive or killed, we are to endure bravely. When things become so dark and painful that it seems the devil has control, God will enable us to persevere in faith (Rev. 13:9-10).

*The blasphemous names* on the beast's seven heads bring to mind our society's blasphemous filth that is being spewed out by television, movies, videos, and so-called contemporary art. This multiheaded beast seems to be gaining, not only in power and influence, but also in acceptance. The dragon, Satan, is behind the beast's power (Rev. 13:2b). The church and organizations opposed to the beast's influence seem powerless to stem the evil tide. In this war of blasphemy, Christians will be conquered (Rev. 13:7), that is, worn down. But their faith in Christ will remain intact, for they know that God is in control and that the days of the beast are numbered.

*The beast's "mortal wound [that] had been healed"* (Rev. 13:3) has been given several interpretations. One relates to Nero. It is said that Nero set fire to Rome so that he could be honored for rebuilding it. Nero blamed the Christians for starting the fire and instigated a series of horrible persecutions against them. Some Christians were immersed in oil and used as human torches; others were thrown to the lions. In A.D. 69, Nero committed suicide. Later, as other persecutions broke out, a rumor spread that Nero had come back to life. During the reign of Domitian toward the close of the century, some people believed that Nero was living again in him. Other views assert that the spirit of Nero will live again even more fiercely in another tyrant who will counterfeit Christ, even to the point of appearing to die and rise again.

## THE BEAST FROM THE EARTH (REV. 13:11-18)

John now sees a second beast. In contrast to the first beast, this one emerges from the earth and has only two little horns. It looks like an innocent lamb and does not have the ferocious qualities of the first beast. But when it speaks, its true character is revealed. Its speech indicates that it is inspired by the dragon (Satan).

The second beast works in close conjunction with the first beast, receiving directions and authority from it. The second beast enforces the edict of the first beast, that all humankind worship it, and induces "the inhabitants of earth," that is, the non-Christian world, to make an image of the first beast. Either through magic, ventriloquism, or the power of the devil, the second beast makes the image speak. This beast is also able to work other signs in order to deceive non-Christians (Rev. 13:13-15).

The second beast carries out the edicts of the first beast by exercising economic control over people. It demands that they identify themselves as followers of the beast by means of a mark. No one without this mark can "buy or sell." Whether this refers to an actual or symbolic mark, we do not know.

Worn on the right hand or the forehead, the beast's mark is in a prominent place so that there can be no mistaking the person's loyalty. The right hand or the forehead may also refer to each person's thinking or philosophy of life or to a person's actions and lifestyle. In other words, individuals are to show in an unmistakable way that they revere and honor the beast. Christians refuse to do this, and the absence of the mark indicates clearly to whom they belong. In a sense, this mark is a devilish parody of the sealing of Christians described in Revelation 7. The sealing was an inward mark of ownership and security. The mark of the beast also indicates ownership. A refusal to obey the beast's edict means a deprivation of the necessities of life; for the Christian, it means death.

The second beast not only works very closely with the first beast but also works for it, carrying out its orders. In the first century, under the regimes of the Roman emperors (who are symbolized by the first beast), the second beast would symbolize the priestly group or religious system that enforced and maintained emperor worship. Throughout the centuries, this beast represents any leaders who work hand in hand with godless governments to divert worship away from the true God. This beast, as we have seen, is also called the "false prophet" (Rev. 16:13; 19:20), indicating that his function is of a religious nature. The deception is insidious and subtle because it looks as innocent as a lamb. Think of the millions of people who have been (and are being) drawn into false religions through the deceitful pleasantries of false prophets. Paul says that the devil disguises himself as an angel of light (2 Cor. 11:14).

*The Number of the Beast*

Many people have speculated on the meaning of the number *666* by which the beast will be recognized. John is using a device known to the Jews as *gematria*. The Greeks used this method also. In the ancient world, the Greeks and Hebrews used the letters of the alphabet to represent numbers. Thus a name could be converted into a number. For instance, the following graffiti has been found on the walls of Pompeii: "I love her whose number is 545." Using this method, people have tried to determine the identity of the beast. They have suggested many names, including Nero and Hitler.

If we agree that six is an incomplete number and implies evil (see p. 8), then we may understand better the meaning of 666. The beast may try to counterfeit Christ by exerting demonic power and demanding to be worshiped, but it will always be a number six—imperfect, incomplete, and evil. It will never attain a number seven, even though it extends itself to a million sixes. The three sixes may also imply a trinity of evil. The fact that 666 is a human number (Rev. 13:18) may indicate that the beast will never be divine and that the antichrist may be a human being.

## PRACTICAL LESSONS FROM THESE CHAPTERS

One main truth from these chapters is the certainty of the existence of a personal adversary, the devil. Nowhere in Scripture is he referred to as an impersonal being or merely an influence. Jesus always refers to Satan as a person, using the pronoun *he*. One of the devil's subtle tactics is to cause people to believe that he does not exist, or to believe that he is merely a bad influence or evil in general. C. S. Lewis, in his book *Screwtape Letters*, gives helpful insights into the reality and duplicity of Satan.

Another important fact to recognize is that Satan is a defeated enemy. What an encouragement it is to Christians who are suffering through the fires of persecution to know that although the devil does his utmost, God is in ultimate control. God has the last word and will provide a way of escape.

What are some ways by which the devil seeks to defeat Christians? He tries to implant lies in the mind by saying, "You haven't really sinned," or "Your sins are too great for God to forgive." If a person has confessed his or her sins and asked for forgiveness, the enemy may bring them back to mind and say, "You're not really forgiven." Satan may try to implant lies about God or the person and work of Jesus Christ. He may try to inject us with feelings of discouragement or depression or distract us with thoughts about illness, death, or suicide. He will use any means to harass Christians and take away their peace.

How may Christians live lives of victory over the enemy? First, we must be aware of his tactics. The Bible tells us that we are not ignorant of his designs (2 Cor. 2:11). Much that plagues us is from the evil one. As Jesus did when tempted (Luke 4:3-13), we must use the word of God against Satan. The following account illustrates how one Christian found release through the power of Christ.

At a church retreat one Saturday evening, the group was discussing the matter of victory over the enemy. One woman told about the vile thoughts that plagued her whenever she was about to receive the Lord's Supper. She had prayed about this, blaming her sinful nature and asking for forgiveness, but found no release. The next morning, before the Communion service, her disturbing thoughts returned. This time, she prayed differently. "If these thoughts are from Satan," she said, "I refuse them in the name of Jesus and by the power of his blood." She stated that she was released immediately and was able to commune with a glad and peaceful heart.

When thoughts and feelings harass us, we can test them in the same way and claim release. Christians are to be warriors, armed with the power of the cross. "But they have conquered him by the blood of the Lamb and by the word of their testimony, for they did not cling to life even in the face of death" (Rev. 12:11). When the devil dangles confessed sins before our eyes and tells us that we are not forgiven, we must remind him of the truth of 1 John 1:9: "If we confess our sins, he who is faithful and just will forgive us our sins and cleanse us from all unrighteousness." Through faith, we can thank God that we are forgiven, even when we do not feel forgiven.

As we pray for others, especially for those who do not know Christ or have not submitted their lives to his lordship, we must realize that the devil aims to keep them from coming to Christ. Paul states in 2 Cor. 4:4, "The god of this world has blinded the minds of the unbelievers, to keep them from seeing the light of the gospel of the glory of Christ." To break his hold over their minds and wills, we need to claim the power of the cross and the name of Jesus against Satan until their eyes are opened to see and respond to the truth of the gospel.

Fighting, we shall be victorious
By the blood of Christ our Lord;
On our foreheads, bright and glorious,
Shines the witness of his Word . . .

"Victory!" our song shall be,
Like the thunder of the sea.

Justus Falckner, 1672–1723
Tr. Emma F. Bevan, 1827–1909

# Lesson 8

# Songs of Victory Await the Faithful

## REVELATION 14–16

Review the outline chart on page 14. Note that we are still in the interlude that occurs between the trumpet judgments in Revelation 8 and 9 and the final series of judgments in Revelation 16.

Read Rev. 14–16. What are your general impressions of this segment? Note how God encourages and warns his people before the bowls of wrath are poured out.

### Study Questions

#### REV. 14:1-5: THE NEW SONG

1. Read Rev. 14:1-5. The scene shifts to heaven, and again we see the 144,000. In chapter 7, they were on earth as the church militant. Here they are in heaven as the church triumphant. God has led them safely home, and not one is missing! In terms of what you see, hear, and feel, what contrasts do you note between this scene and Revelation 12 and 13? Write your observations on a separate piece of paper.

| | Revelation 12–13 | Rev. 14:1-5 |
|---|---|---|
| See | | |
| Hear | | |
| Feel | | |

2. What does the symbolism used here tell us about the redeemed in heaven? about the music?
3. What meaning would this scene (Rev. 14:1-5) have for persecuted Christians on earth? What meaning does it have for you today?

#### REV. 14:6-11: THE MESSAGE OF THE THREE ANGELS

1. Read Rev. 14:6-11. To whom does the first angel bring his message? (v. 6)

a. Recall the meaning of the expression "those who live on the earth." (See p. 68.)
b. What does the angel urge people to do before it is too late? (v. 7)

2. What does the second angel prophesy? (v. 8)
3. The third angel pronounces judgment on those who worshiped the beast and received its mark (vv. 9-11). How did their lives indicate their allegiance to the beast?
4. What does the symbolic language of verses 9-11 tell us about the terrible fate of those who are eternally lost?
5. Do you believe the words in verses 9-11 are true and that hell is an awful reality? If not, why not? If so, what effect should these words have on our attitude toward those who are not Christians?

## REV. 14:12-13: COURAGE AND HOPE FOR CHRISTIANS

1. Read Rev. 14:12-13. What are Christians encouraged to do? (v. 12) Why?
2. Contrast the blessedness of the redeemed (v. 13) with the fate of the lost (vv. 9-11). Note the contrast in how the word *rest* is used in verses 11 and 13.

## REV. 14:14-20: HARVESTTIME

1. Read. Rev. 14:14-20. Note that the final judgment takes place when the harvest is "fully ripe." (See Rev. 14:15, 18.) What does this expression mean? What do you think causes the world to become ripe for judgment?
2. Do you think the United States is ripening for judgment? Why or why not? If so, what can we do to avert judgment? (See 2 Chron. 7:14.)

## REVELATION 15: THE SONG OF MOSES AND THE LAMB

1. Read Rev. 15:1-4. Before the seven angels are permitted to pour out the last plagues, God gives his suffering church another encouraging view of the victorious saints in heaven.
   a. How had these martyrs conquered the beast?

b. Why is their song called the song of Moses and the Lamb? How were their expressions similar to those of the Israelites under pharaoh (Exod. 14–15)?
c. About what do the saints sing? (vv. 3-4)

2. Read Rev. 15:5-8. This paragraph describes the seven angels who come from the glorious presence of God. What is the purpose of their coming?

## REVELATION 16: THE SEVEN BOWLS OF WRATH

1. Read Revelation 16 and note where each of the seven bowls is poured and the result of each. Use a separate piece of paper.

| *Bowl* | *Where Poured* | *Result* |
|---|---|---|
| 1st | | |
| 2nd | | |
| 3rd | | |
| 4th | | |
| 5th | | |
| 6th | | |
| 7th | | |

2. Against whom are these plagues directed? (vv. 2, 9-10) What is the people's response? (vv. 9, 11, 21)
3. How can we say that God's judgments are just? (vv. 5-7)
4. The sixth bowl is different from the others. Note these details:
   a. From where do the demonic spirits come? (v. 13) What is their evil purpose? (v. 14)
   b. Note the words (v. 14b) that refer to the day of the last battle. Whose day is it? What encouragement does this bring as we think about the last conflict between God and the forces of evil?
   c. What do the words in verse 15 mean? Why do you think they are interjected here?
5. Which words in verses 17-21 express the finality and the severity of the last plague?

## PRAYER CONCERNS

List your prayer concerns that have grown out of the study of these chapters. If you are in a group, share these concerns with one another and pray together.

**LESSON 8**
**SONGS OF VICTORY AWAIT THE FAITHFUL**
**REVELATION 14–16**

## Study Helps and Commentary

Judgment began when the seals were opened; more severe judgments followed as the trumpets were blown. Now the bowls of wrath, the final series of judgments, are about to be poured out. In the last lesson (Rev. 12, 13), we saw the reason for the persecution and harassment of the Christians: Satan's hatred for Christ. When the devil was not able to hinder Jesus' great work of redemption, he attacked the followers of the Lamb, causing many of them to be martyred.

According to the closing chapters of the Revelation, the doom of the dragon, the beast, and the false prophet is sure. The bowls of wrath will be poured out on the headquarters of the beast and on all who follow it. This will be a trying time for Christians, and many will be tempted to deny the faith in order to escape persecution. But again, in his tender mercy, God gives John another picture of all the redeemed who have come through persecution victoriously. Like triumphant warriors, they stand with their leader, the Lamb, on the heavenly Mount Zion, singing a new song, the song of Moses and the Lamb.

Before both the seals and the trumpet judgments, Jesus showed John beautiful visions of the redeemed in heaven in order to strengthen the faith of persecuted Christians and to give them hope and courage to endure. Through these glorious visions of heaven, it is as if the Lord is saying to his people, "Be faithful to me. Do not deny me, whatever the cost. Soon you will be with me, singing the triumphant songs of those who have conquered."

### THE NEW SONG (REV. 14:1-5)

Note the contrast between Revelation 14 and 15 and the preceding two chapters:

Here we see the holy angels and the Lamb surrounded by his joyous followers. In Revelation 12 and 13, we saw the three unholy ones—the dragon and the two beasts.

Here we see the mark that identifies those who belong to the Lamb. In Revelation 12 and 13, we saw the mark of the beast.

Here we see beauty, joy, glory, triumph, singing, music, and majesty. In the preceding chapters, we saw fear, deceit, hatred, and blasphemy. We saw people who worshiped the dragon rather than the Lamb, the persecution of the saints, and satanic signs and activity.

In Revelation 12 and 13, we saw from the earthly perspective. In Revelation 14 and 15, we see from the heavenly perspective.

In the Old Testament, *Zion* refers to the city of God, the earthly Jerusalem. Here it refers to the new Jerusalem, heaven itself, and points toward the final victory that is coming when all of history finds its consummation in Christ.

The redeemed have the name of Jesus and the Father on their foreheads. He is their love, their joy, their thought, their all, and he loves them with an everlasting love. He has been with them through every trial, and now they are at home with him, safe and victorious in the Father's house. Every one of them is there. The 144,000 refers to the sum total of all the redeemed. We do not know how many that is, but God knows. He knows the name of every one of his redeemed; not one of his own will be missing.

The song the saints sing is unique, because only forgiven sinners can sing it. Whoever has learned to sing this song of salvation has discovered a new thing: in Christ, the old has passed away and all things have become new. These redeemed ones learned to sing this new song on earth. They chose to renounce their sins, follow Christ, and be loyal to him.

Some commentators interpret Rev. 14:4 literally, saying that this verse refers to a select group of believers who have refrained from marriage. In the Old Testament, however, any form of idolatry or identification with the heathen world was considered whoring and adultery. (See Ezek. 16:23-34.) The Bible does not pronounce a special blessing on those who live a celibate life, nor does it condemn marriage. Perhaps the best commentary on this verse is found in the last part of verse 4: "These follow the Lamb wherever he goes." They have remained loyal to him, refusing to be seduced by the world's enticements or to be deceived by the devil's lies. Just as the path of the Lamb led to the cross, so these people have denied themselves, taken up their cross, and followed him—even unto death. But now they stand before him spotless, rejoicing in his presence.

## THE MESSAGE OF THE THREE ANGELS (REV. 14:6-11)

The first angel (Rev. 14:6-7) comes with the changeless, eternal gospel, pleading with the godless to make use of this last opportunity to repent. He flies in midheaven so that everyone will hear. He pleads with people to turn from the worship of their false gods, whatever they may be. He calls them to worship the only true God, the God of creation who is above all and over all. He reminds them that, even in judgment, God is merciful, for the purpose of the judgments is to call everyone to repentance.

The second angel (Rev. 14:8) pronounces doom on that great seducer of the nations, Babylon. So certain is her fall that the angel speaks as if it has already taken place. The judgment on Babylon will be discussed fully in Revelation 17 and 18.

The third angel (Rev. 14:9-11) enforces the message of the first angel. God, the God of love and mercy, would not have anyone be lost. He sends forth his gospel to all the world, letting people know that he loves them, that he has died for them, and that he wants them with him in the heavenly home. But if they refuse his love and persist in going their own way, worshiping their own gods and clinging to the world's enticements, God must let them have their own way. One aspect of the wrath of God is that God turns the unrepentant over to themselves and their sin. Thus, in a sense, they destroy themselves.

The eternal agony and suffering of the lost is described in Rev. 14:10-11. The words *"in the presence of the holy angels and in the presence of the Lamb"* seem to indicate that an awareness of what the lost have forfeited will intensify their suffering. What agony it will be when those who have rejected Christ and have died without responding to his love look back over their lives and realize that it could have been different. How they will suffer when they contemplate the opportunities they had to yield to Christ that are now lost forever. That which will cause the greatest pain, however, will be the awareness of heaven's blessedness. They will see the angels and the Lamb, the joy and the victory, and will realize that they are eternally shut out from these blessings.

Can we read these tragic words without weeping for those who reject Christ? These words should send us out onto the highways of life with the gracious invitation of the gospel to accept the life that is in Christ Jesus.

## COURAGE AND HOPE FOR CHRISTIANS (REV. 14:12-13)

The doom of those who reject Christ, persecute Christians, and follow the beast should encourage followers of the Lamb to remain faithful to him even though it may mean persecution or death. Should persecution happen, let us remember the beautiful pictures of heaven, where the victorious saints rejoice in the very presence of Jesus. Let us know that God will remember our faithfulness, our labors even to the point of weariness, and our persecutions. All the work we do because of our love for Jesus will follow us into eternity.

## HARVESTTIME (REV. 14:14-20)

In the Gospels, Jesus speaks on several occasions about the end of the age when he will come to separate the chaff from the grain, the sheep from the goats, and gather his elect from the ends of the earth. The final judgment is certain. Rev. 14:14-20 gives us a preview of this judgment, which will be described more fully in later chapters.

The One who sits on a white cloud, wearing a golden crown and wielding a sharp sickle in his hand, is the victorious Christ. Some commentators believe that verses 14-16 refer to the harvest or gathering of Christians and that the second paragraph (Rev. 14:17-20) refers to the judgment on the wicked. Another interpretation holds that Rev. 14:14-16 refers to the general judgment that includes both the righteous and the wicked and that verses 17-20 refer more specifically to the judgment on the unrighteous.

Note that the harvest takes place when the grapes are fully ripe. This indicates that God is in control of history, which is moving steadily toward its end. When the world is ripe for judgment, and only God knows the time, the Messiah will come to execute that judgment. History is not moving along meaninglessly or without direction. Someday God will end present history so that he can bring in his new world order.

We are approaching the final series of judgments, the bowls of wrath. Seven angels stand poised, ready to pour out the final seven plagues. Before this happens, however, the suffering saints, many of whom will be martyred, are permitted to look into heaven. There they see the saints in heaven who conquered the beast and refused every temptation to compromise the truth. The martyrs stood firmly against any edict to worship the state; they were not taken in by the lamblike speech of the false prophet. They followed the Lamb even to death, being martyred for their loyalty to Jesus. Now they stand beside the sea of glass, singing songs of joy to the One who has redeemed them and brought them safely through to victory. Their martyrdom, which seemed to be a victory for the beast, was in truth the beast's defeat and their triumph.

Their triumph reminds us of another such triumph in the Old Testament. God rescued the children of Israel from their beast, the pharaoh, and led them safely and miraculously through the Red Sea. Standing on the shores of that sea, they also sang a song of triumph. (See Exod. 15:1-18.) The martyrs in heaven sing, not only the song of Moses but also the song of the Lamb. This is the song about redemption, the song about the pioneer of their faith who went before them to death and who, through that death, opened the way to glory. As Moses delivered the Israelites from pharaoh, so Jesus will deliver his people from the beast.

The song of the victorious Christians is a song of anticipation. It will be sung after the final consummation, when Christ comes again and "everything that exists in heaven or earth shall find its perfection and fulfillment in him" (Eph. 1:9-10, *Phillips*). As the persecuted Christians on earth see the joyous company of martyrs and hear their songs of triumph, they can project themselves into the picture and know that if they continue to follow the Lamb, even to martyrdom, they, too, will someday join that victorious band.

The seven angels who execute the final judgments are now described (Rev. 15:5-8). Dressed in glorious apparel, they come from the very presence of God. They hold golden bowls that are filled with the wrath of God. This whole scene tells us that the wrath of God results from his holiness, his holy response to sin. God had called to the God-defying world through the seals and trumpet judgments, but the godless people refused to repent. They rejected his offer of love in Christ. Now their cup of iniquity is full. Instead of experiencing God's love, they will experience his wrath.

## THE SEVEN BOWLS OF WRATH (REVELATION 16)

At the direct command of God, the seven angels pour out the wrath of God upon the earth. These judgments are similar to the trumpet judgments (Rev. 8–9), and also resemble the plagues of Egypt.

The first bowl of wrath is directed against those who wear the mark of the beast. Their affliction is like the boils that came upon the Egyptians. This judgment is unlike the first four trumpet judgments in that those judgments did not touch people and were directed against nature.

The second bowl turns the sea into blood. This judgment is similar to the second trumpet judgment, but with this difference: the second trumpet judgment affected only one-third of the sea. Here, the whole sea becomes blood.

The third bowl causes the rivers and springs of water to turn to blood. Similarly, the third trumpet judgment caused a star called Wormwood to fall into one-third of the rivers and springs and make them bitter and poisonous. As a result, many people died. The third bowl of wrath turns all the waters into blood, indicating that more people died from this plague than from the third trumpet judgment.

The beast and its followers had caused much blood to flow by martyring many followers of the Lamb. Now God gives the beast's supporters blood to drink. The angel of the waters proclaims that God's judgment here is just. The altar (which is personified) answers the angel (Rev. 16:7), agreeing that God is righteous and just in sending this plague. The altar may refer to the prayers of the persecuted saints or to the cries of the martyrs (Rev. 6:9) that God would avenge them. God is answering these prayers in the pouring out of the bowls of wrath. He has not forgotten the martyred saints. His judgments are true and just. He is vindicated in his judgments.

The fourth bowl affects the sun, as did the fourth trumpet judgment. But again, the trumpet judgment was partial, darkening one-third of the sun, moon, and stars. This plague is more severe, for it causes intense pain. Note that the sun is "allowed" to scorch people, indicating that God is permitting this painful plague. Those who are scorched realize the hand of God in this, for they curse him for their fate instead of repenting and admitting that they have brought this pain on themselves.

The fifth bowl is directed at the throne or headquarters of the beast, which could refer to Rome as the center of the anti-Christian government in John's day or to the world dominion of antichrist. The plague of darkness intensifies the pain caused by the other plagues, but the evildoers still refuse to repent. They curse God, "gnawing their tongues in agony."

The sixth bowl is different from the others in that it does not cause any pain to the enemies of God. Rather, it dries up the Euphrates River so that the kings from the east may pass over it. The Euphrates, we recall, formed the boundary between Israel and her heathen enemies. The removal of this barrier is symbolically portrayed by the drying up of the river. There are several instances in Scripture, the Red Sea episode being one example, where the drying up of a river indicates God's power.

The unholy trinity—the dragon (the devil), the beast (the anti-Christian political systems), and the false prophet (the anti-Christian religious systems)—angered because of the pain and judgments inflicted on them, determine to wage a final war on the Messiah and his followers. Using demonic power, symbolized by frogs, they influence the kings of the whole godless civilization to join forces with the pagan hordes to make war on Christ and his followers. Their strategy and plans are inspired by hell itself. This bowl calls to mind the sixth trumpet judgment, by which a demonic horde killed one-third of humanity.

Because this final battle will be such a great test for the Christian and will occur suddenly, John interjects, in the name of the Lord, a warning and an encouragement in Rev. 16:15. Just when the battle is at its height and it seems that the cause of the Messiah and his people is being lost, Christ will appear to deliver his own and to defeat every enemy. Therefore, Christians are to keep their eyes on him, loving him and waiting for him. They are not to be taken by surprise knowing that he will come unexpectedly "like a thief" (Rev. 16:15). They are not to sleep but to keep alert for signs of his coming. They are to live each day in his presence, motivated to holy living by the thought, "Perhaps he will come today!"

Armageddon is a term that not only the Christian but also the secular world associates with the final holocaust that will end history. Most scholars believe that Armageddon (sometimes spelled Harmageddon) is derived from the Hebrew word Har Megiddo, meaning Mount Megiddo. But there is no known mountain by that name. However, near Megiddo, which could refer to a mound of a city, was a large, broad valley, the plain of Esdraelon, also known as the valley of Megiddo. Here a number of battles were fought in which God, in miraculous ways, brought victory to his people, Israel. This is the only place in the Bible where the term Armageddon is used, and it is not used again in the Revelation. Since there is no place known by that name, it seems best to regard it as symbolic.

However, there are writers who believe that an actual battle will take place on the plain of Esdraelon in the holy land. The enemy forces led by antichrist will war against the Christian army. At a decisive moment Christ will appear to defeat antichrist and save his people.

Another view holds that Armageddon does not refer to a geographic location or to an armed battle, but to the final struggle between the forces of Christ and those of Satan. When the conflict becomes the fiercest, Christ will appear suddenly to rescue his people and to defeat every enemy.

The seventh bowl is the climax of the series of judgments; it describes the collapse of Babylon, symbolizing the center of anti-Christian world power. To the early Christian, this would undoubtedly refer to Rome, which was the headquarters of the beast (Domitian, the Roman emperor). Eschatologically, however, it refers to "the sum total of pagan culture, social, intellectual, and commercial that had opposed and oppressed the people of God from time immemorial."[1]

The seventh bowl is poured into the air, which scholars say is the abode of demons. (See Eph. 2:2.) The demons are attacked in their own territory. The great voice that calls from out of the temple is God himself, proclaiming from his throne in heaven that the judgments are now completed and that the end of this world has come. All the cataclysmic occurrences in nature symbolize the power, holiness, and glory of God. His wrath—his holiness reacting against sin—is poured out on Babylon, the capital of the beast. An earthquake breaks the city into three pieces, symbolizing the complete collapse of non-Christian culture and civilization.

God remembers Babylon (Rev. 16:19), who had persecuted and killed the followers of the Lamb. God is aware of all their sufferings; he has heard their cries and prayers that his honor would be avenged; he has not forgotten them. Now the time has come. The followers of the beast, who have seen the hand of God at work in the seal and trumpet judgments, refuse to repent. Now they must drain the cup of the fury of God's wrath. Convulsions in nature, including hailstones that weigh as much as one hundred pounds each, do not evoke any kind of repentance. Instead, the enemies of God curse him, thus sealing their eternal fate. The statement, "every island fled away" (Rev. 16:20) perhaps looks ahead to the complete renovation and restoration of the world, when everything in the created order becomes new.

Note that God pours out the bowls of wrath on the beast, its followers, and on its throne. God's children may experience suffering, persecution, and martyrdom, but they will never experience God's wrath. That is reserved for his enemies.

## MESSAGES FROM THE REVELATION TO OUR TIME

*The message to the world is this*: History is moving steadily and surely toward its close. The godless, materialistic world system will collapse. God is in perfect control. Through every means possible, he calls all people to repent. He sends out his gospel to the whole earth. But when people refuse to acknowledge God, when they spurn his love and continue in their sins, then God, after much patience and long-suffering, must let them have their own way and experience his wrath. Jesus affirms this same truth when he says: "Whoever believes in the Son has eternal life; whoever disobeys the Son will not see life, but must endure God's wrath" (John 3:36).

*The message for the Christian is this:* In Christ, your victory is certain. The devil may harass you, suffering and persecution may plague you, and martyrdom may be your lot. But God has not forgotten you. He knows your every trial and is aware of every pain and tear. He is working on your behalf because you are precious to him. Follow the Lamb and be loyal to him. Refuse any temptation to compromise. Be alert to the deceptions of the enemy and keep looking for the return of your Lord. Someday you, too, will join that joyous, victorious multitude, singing the song of Moses and the Lamb.

Am I a soldier of the Cross,
A follower of the Lamb,
And shall I fear to own his cause
Or blush to speak his Name?

Sure I must fight, if I would reign—
Increase my courage, Lord—
I'll bear the toil, endure the pain,
Supported by thy word.

Thy saints, in all this glorious war,
Shall conquer, though they die;
They see the triumph from afar,
By faith they bring it nigh.

When that illustrious day shall rise,
And all thy armies shine
In robes of victory through the skies,
The glory shall be thine.

Isaac Watts, 1674–1748

# Lesson 9

# Only Treasures Rooted in Christ Will Last

## REVELATION 17–18

The Revelation and history itself are moving toward the close of the age, when God will bring in the new heaven and the new earth. But first, every enemy of Christ and his church must be removed.

Review the outline chart on page 14, taking special note of the enemies that have been mentioned in the Revelation thus far and their symbolic meaning.

Read Revelation 17 and 18, which describe the character and destruction of Babylon—the godless world system. Note that in chapter 17, Babylon is depicted as a whore and in chapter 18 as a city.

### Study Questions

REVELATION 17: WHORE BABYLON

1. Read Rev. 17:1-6. How does this description of Babylon indicate her great evil and her hatred of Christians?
   a. Note Babylon's sins.
   b. What does the description of the woman's dress and appearance indicate about the godless world system?
   c. What groups has she seduced? (v. 2)
   d. On what is the woman seated? (v. 3) Where have you seen this beast before? (See Rev. 13:1.) What is its symbolic meaning?
2. Read Rev. 17:7-14. These verses are among the most difficult to understand in the Revelation. Try to answer the following questions with the help of the commentary section and other materials. Do not be discouraged if you cannot understand all the details.
   a. How is the beast that carries the woman described? (vv. 7-8, 11) What are some possible interpretations of the beast's appearance?

b. What do the beast's seven heads symbolize? (vv. 9-10) What are some possible interpretations of this symbolism?
c. What do the ten horns symbolize? (v. 12) What is their relationship to the beast? (v. 13)
d. Notice the expressions that indicate that God is in perfect control and that he limits the rule of the beast to a brief period (vv. 10, 12).
e. Rev. 17:14 looks toward the end of history, when all the forces of evil will unite against Christ and his followers. How may we be certain that the Lamb will be victorious? (Note his title.)
f. Note the words in verse 14 that describe the followers of the Lamb. What do the words indicate about their relationship to the Lamb?

3. Read Rev. 17:15-18, which describe God's judgment of the whore.
   a. How is the extent of the whore's influence and empire indicated? (v. 15)
   b. How will the devotees of the whore treat her? (v. 16)
   c. How does verse 17 show that God is in control and that his purposes will be carried out?
4. Perhaps the first-century Christians saw the debauchery, affluence, and secularism of Rome in the symbolic description of the whore. If John were writing today, how might he describe present-day civilization and culture?

## REV. 18:1-8: DESTRUCTION OF BABYLON

1. Read Rev. 18:1-8. According to verse 3, what is the cause of Babylon's downfall?
2. What is the call to God's people in verse 4? This call is repeated many times in Scripture. Why is there such urgency?
3. Early Christians may have been tempted to compromise with Babylon in order to escape persecution. If they chose to identify with the worldly Babylon, what could they expect? (v. 4)
4. What characterizes Babylon's sins? (vv. 5-8)
5. What do verses 5-8 reveal about God's punishment of Babylon?
6. Read 1 John 2:15-17, which contains the same call as in Rev. 18:4: a warning to keep from becoming identified with the godless world system. For you personally, what is the most subtle temptation from the godless world?

## REV. 18:9-19: THE LAMENTS OF BABYLON'S FOLLOWERS

1. Read Rev. 18:9-10. Name the first people to lament Babylon's destruction.
   a. What has been their relationship to Babylon?
   b. Why do they weep and wail? What has the city meant to them?
2. Read Rev. 18:11-17a. What group now weeps and mourns?
   a. Why does this group weep and mourn?
   b. Note the cargoes that came to affluent Rome, including slaves—human lives (v. 13b). In what ways does modern "Babylon" traffic in human souls?
   c. What has the city meant to the merchants? (vv. 15-16)
3. Read Rev. 18:17b-19. Name the third group that wails over the city.
   a. Why do these people mourn?
   b. How is the suddenness of the city's devastation described? (vv. 10b, 17a, 19b)
4. What common factor causes all this wailing? (See Rev. 18:11, 15, 17a, 19a.) What contemporary applications can you make from their example?

## REV. 18:20: THE CALL TO REJOICE

Read Rev. 18:20. Which people are called on to rejoice? Why?

This verse is a glad, triumphant shout of joy because God's judgments show that he cares about every wrong Christians have suffered.

## REV. 18:21-24: THE FINAL LAMENT OVER BABYLON

1. Read Rev. 18:21-24. How is the final overthrow of Babylon symbolized?
2. What will be found "no more" in the city? Briefly summarize the meaning of each of the six "no mores."
3. Why does God destroy the city? (vv. 23b-24)

## SOME APPLICATIONS

1. Why do you think the godless world system is pictured as both a whore and a city?

2. Is it possible for the Christian to coexist with the "world"? If so, how? Give some examples. If not, why not?
3. What encouragement would these chapters provide for persecuted Christians of any age who have had to forfeit their jobs or lose their possessions because of their faithfulness to Christ?
4. In terms of these chapters, do you think the energy and economic woes that beset the world today may be a blessing in disguise, especially for us in the United States? Why or why not?
5. Which prayer concerns do these chapters bring to mind? Write them down and pray about them. If you are studying with a group, pray about them together.

## LESSON 9
## ONLY TREASURES ROOTED IN CHRIST WILL LAST
## REVELATION 17–18

### Study Helps and Commentary

As the Revelation moves toward its close, we see history move toward its close as well. The bowls of wrath, the final series of judgments, have been poured out on the beast and its followers. After the final bowl of wrath is emptied, the voice of God says, "It is done!" Judgment on the earth is now complete. All that remains for God is to dispose of his enemies: the dragon, the beast, the false prophet, Babylon, and death—the last enemy. Their destruction is described in Revelation 17–20. Their removal makes way for the new heaven and earth, which is the subject of Revelation 21 and 22.

In Rev. 14:8, the fall of Babylon is predicted. The last bowl of wrath to be poured out (Rev. 16:17-21) causes the great city of Babylon to collapse. In Revelation 17 and 18, Babylon and her destruction are described.

Who is Babylon and what does she symbolize? The history of Babylon in the Old Testament can help us understand the symbolic meaning. Babylon was founded after the great flood when the people, in defiance of God, built a high tower so that they could be independent of him (Gen. 11:4). Thus, the tower of Babel (and later Babylon) symbolized pride, defiance of God, a desire to live independently of God, and a rebellious spirit that chose sin in preference to God's laws. To the readers of the Revelation in John's day, all that Babylon stood for in past history was embodied in Rome.

## WHORE BABYLON (REVELATION 17)

Again John is "in the spirit" (v. 3), indicating that another vision is about to unfold before his eyes. In this vision, he is carried into the wilderness, where he sees the figure of a woman seated on a beast. The waters represent "peoples and multitudes and nations and languages" (Rev. 17:15). The beast seems to be the same one that was introduced in Revelation 13 and represents all the world governments and systems that are hostile to Christianity.

The woman is called a *whore*. This term was familiar to Old Testament readers because any idolatry—any unfaithfulness to God on the part of Israel—was spoken of as spiritual adultery or whoredom. The woman is dressed like a whore in lavish and garish attire that is meant to attract followers. Those who are taken in by her extravagant appeal, the kings of the earth and the inhabitants of the earth (secular society), become drunk with her wine. She, too, is drunk with the "blood of the saints and the blood of the witnesses to Jesus" (Rev. 17:6), for she has caused the death of many of God's children.

The woman is another of the devil's allies. Like the other lackeys of Satan, she is a deceiver. Through her glamour, wealth, industry, commerce, and pagan culture, she seeks to seduce the nations of the world away from faith in the true God. She is the spirit of the world that is anti-Christ and anti-God. It was customary in ancient times for prostitutes to identify themselves by means of a headband. This woman has a name of mystery on her forehead, which identifies her as the "mother of whores" (Rev. 17:5). Not only does she entice people away from God, but also she enlists her followers to do the same.

The woman symbolizes the Rome of John's day, which was characterized by affluence, debauchery, crime, immorality, and a hatred for Christianity. However, Babylon symbolizes much more than historical Rome. She symbolizes any non-Christian civilization or system that worships the world, hates Christians, and seeks to seduce people away from God. It is said that astrology was the chief religion in ancient Babylon. Thus the term *Babylon* refers to a secular civilization that wears the facade of religion. Some interpreters believe that Babylon symbolizes the false church that gets its support from anti-Christian governments, as symbolized by the beast on which she rides.

*The Mystery of the Woman and the Beast*

John is amazed at what he sees, so the angel hastens to interpret the meaning of the woman and the beast (Rev. 17:7-18). This explanation is puzzling and difficult to understand. The beast is to be identified with the beast of Revelation 13, for they both have ten horns and seven heads that represent kingdoms and nations that have followed the beast. The beast is said to have existed in the past, *it was*; at the present writing, *it is not*; and in the future, *it is to come* (Rev. 17:8). This explanation also reminds us of the beast of the Revelation 13, who had a mortal wound that had healed. As mentioned earlier, the beast may have reminded the readers of Nero, who persecuted Christians, committed suicide, and was rumored to have come back to life. However, the beast in Revelation 17 is said to "ascend from the bottomless pit" (v. 8). This means that it comes from the place of demonic spirits who are in Satan's power. The passage may mean that the spirit of such leaders as Nero, Domitian, Mao, Stalin, and others who have done the devil's work in their hatred of Christians will at the end of the age culminate in the person of antichrist, who will be Satan incarnate.

Every civilization and ruler who has defied and tried to eradicate Christianity has been defeated. But other God-defying systems that have the same spirit of hatred for the Lamb and his followers continually rear their heads. They will go down to perdition once and for all, however. (Their doom is described in Revelation 19.) The angel states that the godless and those without salvation (those "whose names have not been written in the book of life") will marvel when they see the beast revived time and time again in history (Rev. 17:8). At the end of the age, they will not only marvel but also pay homage and follow it, not realizing that its doom and theirs are certain.

Wisdom is needed to understand Rev. 17:9-14. The seven heads of the beast may represent the seven mountains on which the woman is seated. This would seem to refer to Rome, for tradition says that

Rome was built on seven hills. But the heads are also seven kings (Rev. 17:9-10), which could refer to rulers or kingdoms that have been hostile to Christianity. Five are in the past; one, Rome, was in power when John wrote; and one is to come. This coming ruler could refer to the last world emperor through whom the antichrist will wield power.

"The beast that was and is not, it is an eighth but it belongs to the seven" (Rev. 17:11) is perhaps one of the most difficult verses in the Revelation. It may mean that, following a succession of rulers who are hostile to Christianity and are in reality antichrists, an eighth ruler will emerge who is like the others in hatred of Christ, yet is unique and distinct from them.

The ten kings symbolized by the ten horns (Rev. 17:12) have been the subject of much discussion. They had not yet appeared on the scene when John wrote the Revelation. Some, who interpret the Revelation literally, believe that when ten nations joined the European Common Market, the reference to the ten kings was fulfilled. Isbon Beckwith believes that the kings are "purely eschatological figures representing the totality of the power of all nations on the earth which are to be made subservient to Antichrist."[1]

*Hope for Christians*

Into the darkness of this picture, John interjects a light of hope and courage for the tried and tested Christian (Rev. 17:14). The Lamb will conquer the beast and its cohorts. He is "Lord of lords" and "King of kings." All those who oppose him will last but an hour; none can stand before him. Therefore, let the Christian continue to be faithful to the Lamb. Even though it may seem that the forces of Satan are winning, Christ will be the ultimate victor, and all who belong to Christ will share his victory.

In Rev. 17:15-18 John returns to the subject of the whore. In the previous paragraph (vv. 9-14), most of the discussion centered on the beast. The whore, as we have seen, is seated on waters that represent "peoples and multitudes and nations and languages." This indicates her worldwide influence. She seems to have been very successful. Through her allure, glamour, fascination, power, and religious facade, she has influenced the whole world to follow her and to idolize materialistic values. In his first letter, John characterizes her influence using the words "the desire of the flesh, the desire of the eyes, the pride in riches" (1 John 1:16). Every anti-Christian government has promoted her ideology.

But now we see a surprising development. The powers that have been supporting the whore—the beast and the ten horns—turn on her and destroy her. One interpretation of this passage is that the revived Nero comes with his Parthian cohorts and destroys Rome. Perhaps, however, this event has more far-reaching implications than historical Rome. The godless, materialistic civilization that Satan and his cohorts direct, organize, and propagate for one purpose—to oppose God and his kingdom—will continue only as long as God permits. Therefore, it is rushing toward destruction. In a mysterious way, God seems to permit evil to destroy itself; the beast will turn on its own ally, the whore.

Is this not, in a sense, happening today in the ecology and energy crisis, in fascination with military weapons, in the lust for power and material things? Human beings are destroying themselves and their world.

Is this not also true on a personal level? An individual who drinks the world's wine and lives solely on the physical, materialistic level soon discovers that life loses its meaning. Many such people end their lives in desperation. On a broader level, this passage is saying that the whole God-defying, secular civilization will one day be destroyed in order to make way for God's new world where righteousness will reign.

## THE DESTRUCTION OF BABYLON (REV. 18:1-8)

The identity, character, and influence of Babylon—the whore—is described in Revelation 17. Chapter 18 portrays her destruction and the lament of her devotees. The angel echoes the words another angel uttered in Rev. 14:8: "Fallen, fallen is Babylon the great!" Again this event is stated in the past tense, as if it has already taken place.

We must keep in mind that John is describing here the collapse of eschatological Babylon, the complete destruction of the godless civilization that will take place at the end of the age. The words that the writer uses to describe the utter devastation of Babylon are taken from Isaiah (e.g., 2:19) and Jeremiah (chapters 50–51), which pronounce the doom of Babylon and Nineveh. These prophecies literally have been fulfilled in relation to these cities. Through the centuries, Babylon has remained uninhabited (Rev. 18:2), but in 1991 it made headlines with the news that Saddam Hussein was restoring the ancient city.

In Rev. 18:3, John gives the cause of Babylon's destruction. Babylon's one driving aim has been to draw people away from worshiping the true God to worshiping the beast. To do this, she has used the seductive powers of a whore and the glamour and wealth of a city. The nations of the world and the "merchants of the earth" believed her lies, drank her wine, and became infatuated with her riches and pleasures.

A voice of warning sounds (Rev. 18:4). God calls his people to separate themselves from Babylon, because if they identify with her, they will also experience her plagues. The severe persecution and resultant martyrdom of many followers of the Lamb might tempt Christians to affiliate with Babylon in order to escape. But the warning here is to remember the certain doom of Babylon and all her followers. God has always called his people to come out and be separate from the world.

The justice of God's judgment on Babylon is revealed (Rev. 18:5-8). Babylon has defied God, martyred the saints, and tricked the world into believing that people can get along very well without God. She has lived in self-indulgence, luxury, and praise, boasting, "I rule as a queen; I am no widow, and I will never see grief" (18:7). But God has not forgotten her sins or her treatment of his beloved children. Her self-deification has accumulated the wrath of God. Suddenly, in a single hour, she will be brought down from her arrogant perch and completely devastated. She has caused Christians great suffering and will be repaid in double measure. Plagues, pestilence, mourning, and famine will ruin her. Her doom is certain because God is just. "You reap whatever you sow," says Paul (Gal. 6:7). God is mighty; he is able to bring Babylon to utter ruin.

## THE LAMENTS OF BABYLON'S FOLLOWERS (REV. 18:9-19)

*The kings of the earth* are the first to lament Babylon's ruin (Rev. 18:9-10). They have been taken in by her lies, believing that worldly power, materialistic success, and technological advances would guarantee their security and success. Now, as they see the object of their affections going up in smoke, they realize it was all a lie. They have been duped. Standing at a distance, terrified by her torment, they utter their doleful dirge: "Alas, alas, the great city Babylon, the mighty city!"

*The merchants of the earth* are the next to join the chorus of dirges (Rev. 18:11-17a). They weep and mourn because their businesses have failed. The bottom has dropped out of the market. Their grief is entirely selfish, for they weep not so much for the city as for what its destruction has done to them.

The list of items that make up the cargo (vv. 12-13) indicates the luxury and extravagance of the wares that found their way from distant places to Rome. There were precious stones, silk from China (it was said that silk was so expensive that a pound cost a pound of gold), sweet-smelling spices from the East, wood and ivory, and slaves (literal translation is bodies) from any country that would supply them.

The opulent, self-indulgent way of life that characterized ancient Rome is well documented by historians. Her destruction prefigures the eschatological destruction of the great city Babylon. All the merchants of the earth—all people who have invested heavily in the cargoes of this world, forgetting that only heavenly treasures will last—will one day realize their folly. Nothing was intrinsically wrong with most of their wares. All of them, except the slaves, were beautiful gifts of God, meant to enhance life and bring joy. But Babylon used them to entice people away from God. The merchants succumbed to her wiles, making the wares their god.

What a tragedy! The godless people had looked to material success to satisfy them and give them the good life. Now they realize that it has all evaporated; the splendors of Babylon are lost forever (Rev. 18:14). Like the kings of the earth, the merchants stand far off, watching sadly as Babylon falls to her ruin but not lifting a finger to help. They had no real love for Babylon; only the wealth Babylon brought to the merchants bound them to her. In their lament (Rev. 18:15-17a), they admit that all the glamour, beauty, and wealth that characterized Babylon, the whore, was but a facade. Nothing was there of eternal value. Now they are bankrupt; that on which they had pinned their hopes is gone forever.

Next the shipmasters, seafarers, and sailors raise their voices and join the lament (Rev. 18:17b-19). In oriental fashion, they show their grief by throwing dust on their heads. Like the merchants, their sorrow is purely selfish. They cry, not for the ruined city itself but because they can no longer grow rich from her wealth.

## THE CALL TO REJOICE (REV. 18:20)

A note of triumphant praise is now interjected into the series of doleful laments. The saints, apostles, and prophets are called on to praise God, for now all the outrages against Christ and his children have been avenged. Babylon the great, the enemy of God and persecutor of his people, has been destroyed. Now God can bring in the new heaven and the new earth, peopled by those who have been made new in Christ.

## THE FINAL LAMENT OVER BABYLON (REV. 18:21-24)

Whereas the business and commercial interests in the world uttered the previous laments, an angel pronounces this final lament. The angel symbolizes the complete and final destruction of the God-defying world system as he hurls a huge stone like a millstone into the depths of the sea, from which it can never rise. In similar fashion, after reading from a scroll that recorded the prophecy of the destruction of historical Babylon, Seraiah was to hurl the scroll into the Euphrates (Jer. 51:59-64).

There is sadness and tragedy in that haunting refrain "no more," which is repeated six times. It is as if the angel is contemplating what could have been, the glory that could have belonged to Babylon had she not turned from God and used all her powers to seduce others away from him. There seems to be an ascending climax in the use of the words "*no more.*" No more music, no more artisans, no one to grind wheat to sustain life, no more light (only utter darkness), no more love relationships or the joys of family life. All the things mentioned could have enhanced and beautified life, but now they are stripped away. Those who have followed Babylon are left bereft, bankrupt, and eternally desolate.

Again, the reason for Babylon's destruction is given (Rev. 18:23b-24). She promoted business tycoons who were full of arrogance and pride. She seduced the nations of the world into thinking that they could manage without God and that living on the materialistic level meant happiness and success. Finally, she was responsible for the martyrdom of countless of God's faithful followers, not only in Rome but all over the earth.

## BABYLON TODAY

As we contemplate John's descriptions of Babylon, we are struck by many similarities to our world today. Babylon is still with us and will remain with us until she is destroyed at the second advent of Christ. Let's consider some of the marks of contemporary Babylon.

*Between the nations of the world.* Babylon is with us in nuclear weapons, terrorism, distrust among nations, lust for power, war, planning and seeking peace without God, and depending on technology rather than on God for security.

*Within society.* Babylon is evident in our lust for things, pleasure madness, crime, corruption, drugs, immorality, and hard-core pornography. The late historian and columnist Max Lerner said, "We're living in a Babylonian society, perhaps more Babylonian than Babylon itself."

*In religion and the church.* Babylon influences the growing interest in the cultic religions that attract thousands of followers and false religions that deny the deity and vicarious atonement of Jesus Christ, the tendency among some churches to emphasize social action and community outreach to the exclusion of the preaching of the gospel, the tendency of other churches to become so ingrown and concerned with their survival that they are blinded to the needs of others, and the temptation for the church to imitate and adopt the world's methods of success rather than to rely on the power of the Holy Spirit.

*On the personal level.* Babylon leads us to become too enamored with the world—permitting things to play too important a role in life, being infected with the thinking and philosophy of the world, compromising truth and ethical behavior in order to succeed, planning without God, and being proud.

All these—and more—are the marks of Babylon.

*How Should a Christian Live in a Babylonian Society?*
Jesus said that we are to be *in* the world but not *of* it. John wrote, "The love of the Father is not in those who love the world" (1 John 2:15). The call to each of us in Rev. 18:4 is to come out of Babylon and have no part in her sins. We are to be salt and light that will permeate society. We are to work for the redemption of society. We must constantly be on our guard, lest we be seduced by Babylon's glamour, and we must remember that her days are numbered. The entire, godless world system will collapse one day. Let us lay up for ourselves treasures in heaven, remembering that only what is done for Christ will have eternal significance.

O Jesus, I have promised
To serve you to the end;
Remain forever near me,
My master and my friend.
I shall not fear the battle
If you are by my side,
Nor wander from the pathway
If you will be my guide.

Oh, let me feel you near me;
The world is ever near.
I see the sights that dazzle,
The tempting sounds I hear.
My foes are ever near me,
Around me and within;
But, Jesus, then draw nearer
To shield my soul from sin.

John Ernest Bode, 1816–1874

# Lesson 10

## Christ Is King of Kings and Lord of Lords

### REVELATION 19–20

Think through the Revelation and review its songs. Find one song in each of the following chapters: 4, 5, 7, 11, 14, 15, 19. Write down your findings using these headings:

Chapter, Who Sings, To Whom, Theme of Song

Glance at the outline chart of the Revelation on page 14 and note that the three series of judgments are over and that God's great cleansing has begun. What was the first enemy to be eliminated? (Revelation 17–18) Which enemies are eliminated in Revelation 19 and 20?

How many contrasts can you find between the last lesson (Revelation 17–18) and Revelation 19? Think in terms of the two women, the groups, the songs, and the mood. You may wish to come back to this question after you study chapter 19.

#### Study Questions

REV. 19:1-8: THE HALLELUJAH CHORUS

1. Read Rev. 19:1-8. How many hallelujahs do the heavenly choirs sing?
   a. Who sings the first two hallelujahs?
   b. What is the reason for this outburst of song? (v. 2)
2. Who joins in the triumphant song on the third hallelujah? (v. 4) What does their "amen" indicate?
3. Who are invited next to join this universal song of praise? (v. 5)
4. Who sings the fourth hallelujah? (v. 6)
   a. How would you describe this music? (Note "like the sound of . . ." in verse 6.)
   b. What are the two reasons for this song of praise? (vv. 6-8) (Each reason is preceded by the word *for* in the *NRSV*.)

5. In what ways is this hallelujah chorus a climax to all the songs in the Revelation?

## REV. 19:7-10: THE MARRIAGE SUPPER OF THE LAMB

1. Read Rev. 19:7-10. What do you think the marriage supper of the Lamb means? Who is the bride? the Bridegroom? Who is invited?
2. Contrast the clothing of the bride (v. 8) with that of the whore (Rev. 17:4; 18:16). What does this contrast reveal?

## REV. 19:11-16: THE TRIUMPH OF THE KING OF KINGS

1. Read Rev. 19:11-16. These verses leave no doubt as to the identity of this rider on a white horse; it is our triumphant Lord Jesus! List everything stated about Christ in this symbolic description. Then try to state them in your own words. Where have you read some of these descriptions before?
2. Who accompanies Christ when he comes again? Who are they?
3. Some Bible scholars have interpreted the "robe dipped in blood" as referring to judgment—the blood of Christ's enemies. It may also refer to the blood of the atonement. If so, why is it significant that Jesus' robe is sprinkled with blood and his armies' robes are pure white?
4. Why would this vision of the conquering Christ encourage afflicted believers?

## REV. 19:17-21: THE DEFEAT OF THE BEAST AND THE FALSE PROPHET

1. Read Rev. 19:17-21. Contrast the supper of the lost (Rev. 19:17-18) with the marriage supper of the Lamb.
2. Note the groups that will attend the supper of the lost (v. 18). Compare this with Rev. 6:15. What do you notice?
3. What forces gather to make war against Christ? (v. 19)
   a. What is the outcome of the conflict? (vv. 20-21)
   b. What weapon does Christ use to defeat the enemy? (19:15) What is the meaning of this weapon? Why does it bring defeat?

4. Every person will take part in one of the two suppers mentioned in this chapter. According to our study of Revelation, how can we be certain that we will attend the marriage supper of the Lamb?

## REV. 20:1-10: EVERY ENEMY DEFEATED

Chapter 20 is another difficult chapter in the Revelation. We must approach it with humility and a willingness to listen and learn.

1. Read Rev. 20:1-3. What names are given to the dragon? Where was he bound? Why? What may this binding of Satan symbolize? (It is well to remember that throughout the Revelation Satan never has free reign. God always controls and restrains him.)
2. What do you learn from John's vision about the state of the martyrs? (Rev. 20:4-6) What would this vision of the martyrs mean to persecuted, first-century Christians?
3. Read pages 132–35 in the commentary that follows. What are some possible interpretations of the first resurrection (Rev. 20:5) and of the one thousand years?
4. Read Rev. 20:7-10. When will Satan be released?
    a. What will he do when he is set free? (vv. 8-9) It seems that God will use him to usher in the end of the age. God is in control.
    b. How is the vastness of the wicked hosts who oppose God in the final battle symbolized?
    c. Against whom do they direct their attack?
    d. If the city of Babylon symbolizes the godless world system that is opposed to God, what might the "beloved city" symbolize?
    e. What happens to Satan? Who else is with him? How do you react to this?

## REV. 20:11-15: THE FINAL JUDGMENT

1. Read Rev. 20:11-15. Try to visualize the solemnity of this scene. To what are your eyes drawn first?
2. Who will stand before the great white throne? (vv. 12-13)
3. On what basis will the dead be judged? Is this a contradiction to salvation by faith alone? (See James 2:26.) Why or why not?

4. Name all the enemies that are now cast into their eternal place. (Include the three mentioned in verses 14-15.)
5. What is the meaning of the term *the book of life*? How can you be sure that your name is in the book of life? (See 1 John 5:12; John 5:24.) Are you sure that your name is there?

## SING HALLELUJAH!

Someone has called the hallelujah chorus of Revelation 19 "the wedding march of the church." What do you think is meant by this?

Listen to a recording of the "Hallelujah Chorus" from Handel's *Messiah*. As you do so, praise God for that day when sin and evil will be no more and Christ will indeed be King of kings, and Lord of lords!

# LESSON 10
# CHRIST IS KING OF KINGS AND LORD OF LORDS
# REVELATION 19–20

### Study Helps and Commentary

Before God can usher in the new heaven and the new earth, he must eliminate every enemy and all who refuse to have a part in his kingdom. In the last lesson, we witnessed the downfall of Babylon and heard the laments of those who had put all their trust in godless, materialistic values. They wail and mourn because the collapse of Babylon has left them destitute. In contrast to these dirges, we hear the hallelujahs of the celebration in heaven because God has destroyed Babylon, the great enemy of God's people (Revelation 19). Revelation 19 and 20 move toward the climax of the book as every enemy of God is defeated.

## THE HALLELUJAH CHORUS (REV. 19:1-8)

All of heaven sings this mighty song of praise to God because he has demolished Babylon and set his people free from her tyranny. Four times we hear the word *hallelujah*, a Hebrew word that means "praise ye Jehovah." This word is used often in Old Testament songs of praise, especially in the Psalms, but Revelation 19 is the only place where "hallelujah" is used in the New Testament.

John emphasizes truths through the use of contrast. The purpose of this section is to once again bring courage and hope to Christians in the midst of their trials. Following scenes of gloom and doom, John presents visions of glory and victory. In Revelation 18, the whore is central; in Revelation 19, the bride is central. In Revelation 18, there is sin, sorrow, corruption, moaning, doom, and death—all viewed from the perspective of the earth. In Revelation 19, there is righteousness, joy, purity, singing, victory, and life—all viewed from the perspective of heaven.

The first group to take up the song is *a great multitude in heaven* (Rev. 19:1), perhaps the angels. They are filled with ecstasy as they shout out their hallelujahs, praising God for the great work he has done. They give God all the glory, for his work alone has brought salvation and complete deliverance of his people. To him belong power and glory. The angels rejoice that the great worldly seducer, Babylon, the Whore, is now destroyed. It was she who, with her glamour and dazzle, enticed people away from God. It was she who deceived people into making a god of this world, leading them to worship the beast. It was she who caused the suffering and death of countless Christians. Now she is no more. God has answered the prayers of the saints and martyrs. She can no longer harass and harm God's dear children. She has gone up in smoke, destroyed forever.

*The twenty-four elders and the four living creatures* (Rev. 19:4) now join the victory song with their "hallelujah," adding their "Amen" to the song of the angels.

*A voice from the throne* (Rev. 19:5), perhaps one of the cherubim, exhorts everyone on earth to praise God for this great victory.

*Now the whole company of heaven* bursts into song (Rev. 19:6). "Hallelujah!" they exult. They praise the Lord, for now he has taken complete control and will assert his power to bring to consummation the intended purpose of his creation. Now that Babylon is destroyed, the marriage supper of the Lamb can take place. The Old Testament writers often referred to Israel as the wife of the Lord (Jer. 2:2). Paul referred to the church as being the bride of Christ (Eph. 5:25-27, 32).

## THE MARRIAGE SUPPER OF THE LAMB (REV. 19:7-10)

This event, for which the church is longing and waiting, refers to the union of Christ with his bride, the church, when he comes again. In the present time, the church is united with him through faith. She has been given her wedding dress, which is the righteousness of Christ. As she waits for him to come and claim her, she continues to prepare herself for this great event with a life of service, loyalty, love, and devotion (Rev. 19:8). When Christ comes, the Bridegroom and his bride, the church, will be united forever in the new heaven and the new earth.

Small wonder that the whole company of heaven—the Old and New Testament saints and martyrs and every child of God on earth—are called upon to join in this great hallelujah chorus. Handel echoes the victory and triumph of this scene beautifully in the "Hallelujah Chorus" in his *Messiah*.

*The angel now pronounces a blessing* on those who are invited to the marriage supper (Rev. 19:9). This blessing includes not only the invitation but also its acceptance. Only those who respond to the invitation by acknowledging their sin and need, by accepting the wedding garment of forgiveness and Christ's righteousness, and by keeping the oil of the Holy Spirit in their lives will have the privilege of participating in the great marriage supper of the Lamb.

What a joy it will be to have fellowship with Abraham, Sarah, Isaac, Rebekah, Jacob, Rachel, and all the other Old Testament heroes of faith and with Matthew, Mark, Luke, John, Mary, Martha, Lazarus, Paul, Timothy, and scores of New Testament saints and martyrs! John is so overwhelmed at the prospect of this joyous gathering that he falls prostrate before the angel. Perhaps he thinks the voice he hears is that of Christ or God. However, the angel puts himself on the same level as John and other Christians in the matter of worship. He states emphatically that God is the only One to be worshiped.

## THE TRIUMPH OF THE KING OF KINGS (REV. 19:11-16)

At last the climactic moment in history has arrived. Christ comes again to defeat every foe and to bring to fulfillment the kingdom of God on earth. In the previous paragraph (Rev. 19:9-10), the marriage supper of the Lamb was promised but was not actually described. Here the union of the heavenly Bridegroom with his bride, the church, is fulfilled.

Until this point in the Revelation, is has seemed as if the enemies of God were in control. The seal and trumpet judgments and bowls of wrath brought disaster to the earth. The beast was permitted to make war on the saints and to conquer them (Rev. 13:7). Countless Christians have been persecuted and martyred. Yet, God has been in control all along. These enemies exist only as long as God permits. At last he openly asserts his control. From this point on in the Revelation, we see him defeating every enemy to make way for the new heaven and the new earth.

As heaven is opened, John is given a vision of the returning, conquering Christ. In Revelation 4, a door was opened into heaven and John saw God on the throne and Jesus the Lamb holding the scroll of destiny. The contents of the scroll have come to pass, and God's redemptive purposes in history have been fulfilled. Now Christ comes to consummate all of history himself.

*He comes as a warrior*, riding on a white horse that symbolizes victory. There is no doubt as to the identity of this rider. The titles that are ascribed to him, his appearance, and his actions all tell us that Christ himself is returning in power and victory. We saw another rider on a white horse in Revelation 6. That horseman also rode forth as a warrior but sought to conquer people's minds through deceit and evil. It was associated with war, famine, and death.

*He is called "Faithful and True."* He is absolutely dependable and trustworthy. We can confidently stake our lives and our eternal destiny on him. In him, we meet ultimate reality. What a contrast between him and the beast who leads all who follow it to eternal destruction.

*He has eyes like a flame of fire*, looking into the innermost heart, evaluating attitudes and motives.

*He comes as the King wearing many royal crowns.* Jesus is the King now, but it is not evident to most of the world. When he returns in glorious splendor, the whole world will know that he is King of kings and Lord of lords, and those who have followed the beast will realize that the crowns of the beast were but cheap counterfeits.

*The name of Jesus is one that no one knows but Christ himself* (Rev. 19:12). There are hidden mysteries in the person of Christ that the human mind cannot fathom. He is called "Faithful and True," which in a measure we can understand. He is also called "The Word of God" (Rev. 19:13). John uses this same term, *Word* or *logos*, in his Gospel. It means that Jesus reveals and expresses perfectly God's innermost character and message.

*Jesus' garments are dipped in blood* (Rev. 19:13). Some commentators believe this refers to the blood of his defeated enemies. More likely, however, it refers to the blood of Calvary, for the Lamb conquers through his death.

*As he rides forth, he is accompanied by an army* of heavenly beings (Rev. 19:14) who are dressed in white and also ride white horses. Some interpreters believe that this army represents the saints and martyrs in heaven. Others believe they are angels. Jesus spoke of angels accompanying him when he returns: "When he comes in the glory of his Father with the holy angels" (Mark 8:38). However, this army does not seem to be equipped for battle. Jesus alone fights this battle. With the sword of his mouth, which is the word of God, he smites the nations (Rev. 19:15). This word is not the gospel; it is a terrible word of judgment.

Just as God brought the world into being with the word, he now brings history to a close with the word. This is the only weapon Christ uses. With the word, he ends the hell that people have made of his world. In describing this, John uses Ps. 2:9, which vividly portrays the power of the messianic King: "You shall break them with a rod of iron, and dash them in pieces like a potter's vessel."

The second coming of Christ will be a terrible and fearful event for those who rejected him, followed Babylon, and worshiped the beast. The first coming of Christ holds no fear for the unbelieving world; gladly people join in celebrating the birth of the lovely Child in the manger. But the world will not celebrate Christ's second coming. When he rides forth triumphantly to cleanse his world in preparation for the new world, all will know unmistakably that he is King of kings and Lord of lords. Then "every knee should bend, in heaven and on earth and under the earth, and every tongue should confess that Jesus Christ is Lord, to the glory of God the Father" (Phil. 2:10-11).

## THE DEFEAT OF THE BEAST AND THE FALSE PROPHET (REV. 19:17-21)

Even before the great battle between Christ and antichrist begins, an angel, standing in the sun where he can be seen by all the birds of prey, invites the vultures to feast on the flesh of all those who have rejected Christ. What a contrast between this supper of God and the marriage supper of the Lamb! The marriage supper brings visions of rejoicing, victory, fellowship, and love in the presence of the Bridegroom throughout all eternity. The supper of God described here, however, brings utter tragedy, despair, alienation, and hopelessness forever.

The participants in the battle now assemble. The beast and the kings of the earth, symbolizing the anti-Christian political and military world system headed by antichrist, gather their forces to make war on the Messiah. The battle itself is not described. The emphasis is on the decisive victory of Christ over antichrist. The beast and the false prophet—the two beasts of Revelation 13—are both captured and thrown alive into the lake of fire. The false prophet represents the priestly system that enforced emperor worship during the reign of Domitian. In a broader sense, the false prophet represents all religions and philosophies that deny and reject the person and work of Christ. When Christ comes again, every religious and political system, every nation, and every individual who refuses to bow before Christ and acknowledge him as Savior and Lord will be given what has been chosen—separation from God forever.

## EVERY ENEMY DEFEATED (REV. 20:1-10)

Before looking into the meaning of chapter 20, let us summarize the events as they are presented. Satan is bound for a thousand years (Rev. 20:1-3). At the beginning of this period, the saints and martyrs are resurrected and reign with Christ (Rev. 20:4-6). At the end of this period, Satan is set free and the enemies of God make war on Christ and his saints. Christ defeats them, and Satan is thrown into the lake of fire where the beast and the false prophet have also been thrown (Rev. 20:7-10). Finally, we see the great white throne, where each individual will be judged and his or her final destiny will be sealed. Death and Hades are thrown into the lake of fire, along with those whose names are not written in the Lamb's book of life (Rev. 20:11-15). Everything is now ready for the new heaven and new earth.

*The Millennium*

The literal meaning of the word *millennium* is a period of a thousand years. Although not actually used in Revelation 20, we use millennium to refer to the thousand-year reign of Christ. The thousand-year reign of Christ has become a subject of great interest and controversy. We will look at three interpretations of the millennium.

*The postmillennial view* holds that the millennium does not refer to a literal thousand years but symbolizes the whole age from the coming of Christ to his coming again. During this time, the church will grow and Christianity will have such a great influence on the world that most people will become Christians. Evil will be subdued (the devil bound), righteousness will triumph, and the golden age of the kingdom of God will be ushered in. Then Christ will come. Christ comes *after* the symbolic millennium, hence the term *postmillennialism* is used.

*The premillennial view* holds that Christ will come *before* the thousand-year period and will reign a thousand years on earth. The thousand years is usually taken literally, but it may refer to an ideal time, long or short. Premillennialists believe that the Revelation describes a chronological series of events relating to the second coming of Christ that should be interpreted as literally as possible. The first event is the "rapture" of the church (a Greek word meaning "to be caught up"). Christians and resurrected believers will meet the Lord in the air when he comes for them. Some interpreters say that this will be a "secret" rapture—people will disappear with no indication of what happened.

According to this view, the marriage supper of the Lamb follows the rapture (Rev. 19:7-9). While the glorified church is rejoicing with Christ in heaven, the great tribulation takes place on earth under the reign of the antichrist. Following this period of suffering, Christ comes again, this time *with* his saints. Satan is bound for a thousand years and his power curbed so that he cannot deceive the nations. Christ reigns on earth with his saints for a thousand years and enforces righteousness. At the end of this period, Satan is set free to deceive the nations again and to gather all the enemies of God to battle against Christ and his people. But Christ defeats the enemy, and the devil is thrown into the lake of fire where the beast and the false prophet have already been thrown. Then follows the resurrection of the unbelieving dead.

The premillennial view holds to two resurrections, the resurrection of believers before the thousand-year period and the resurrection of the unsaved after the millennium is over. After the judgment at the great white throne, the new heaven and new earth are ushered in.

The premillennial view (dispensationalism) is about 160 years old. It began in England and spread to the United States, where it found ready acceptance. Cyrus I. Scofield adopted it and used it in his *Scofield Reference Bible.* An author who has done a great deal to popularize this view is Hal Lindsey, with his book, *The Late Great Planet Earth.* Biblical scholars who do not agree with this approach believe that the premillennial dispensational interpretation violates the true meaning of the biblical text. Yet writers and teachers such as Lindsey have alerted people to the importance of being ready for Christ's second coming at any time. The premillennial view emphasizes the imminent return of Christ more than the other views.

Premillennialists do not completely agree on the order of events. The following diagram represents a view held quite generally.

**PREMILLENNIAL VIEW**

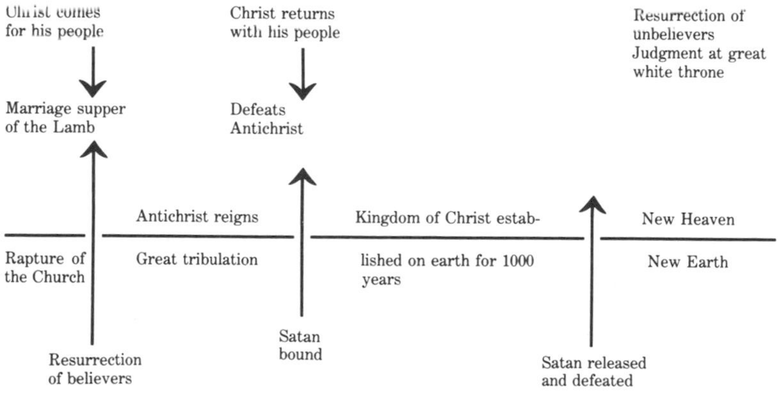

Christ comes for his people
Marriage supper of the Lamb
Rapture of the Church
Resurrection of believers
Christ returns with his people
Defeats Antichrist
Antichrist reigns
Great tribulation
Satan bound
Kingdom of Christ established on earth for 1000 years
Satan released and defeated
Resurrection of unbelievers
Judgment at great white throne
New Heaven
New Earth

*The amillennial view* holds that there is no literal millennium and that the thousand years symbolize the entire time that the church exists on earth. This view denies that there will be either a period of righteousness and peace, as set forth by postmillennialism, or a personal and visible reign of Christ on earth with the saints, as set forth by premillennialism. Amillennialism teaches that good and evil—the kingdom of God and the kingdom of Satan—develop simultaneously and grow until the end of this age. At the second coming of Christ, the resurrection and judgment will take place and be followed by the new heaven and new earth.

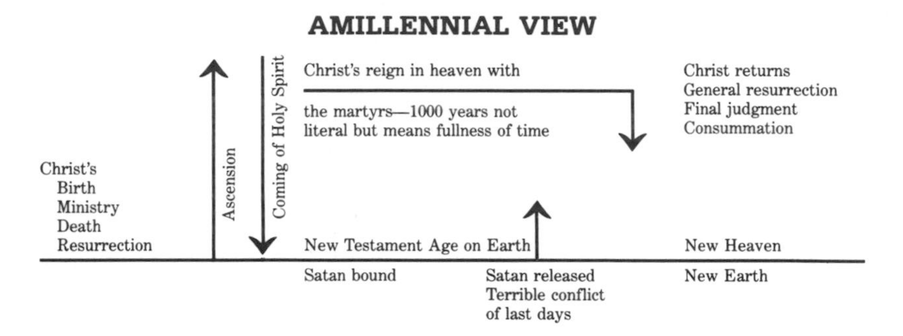


*How Shall We Evaluate These Views?*
Only God has answers to the many questions relating to the end of time. We must be content to leave the working out of the details to him.

Although sincere biblical scholars are identified with each of the three views, the most widely held view is the amillennial view, which is as old as Christianity. Since the early years of the church, amillennialism has been the most widely accepted view and is the only view either expressed or implied in the great historical confessions of the church.

It is most important to remember that our interpretation of the millennium does not affect our salvation. Furthermore, we must be on our guard lest we become so fascinated with details that we miss the blessing of the message in this book. We must also watch, lest we adopt an attitude of dogmatic certainty that says, "This is the way things will happen. This is the order of events." Almost certainly surprises are in store for all of us.

*Other Details*
*The binding of Satan* for a thousand years (Rev. 20:1-3) is interpreted by *amillennialists* to mean that Christ's death and resurrection

broke the power of Satan. They teach that he is bound now in the lives of Christians to the degree that, by God's grace, they yield their lives to the Holy Spirit's control. Satan's power is curbed, not only in the lives of Christians but also in the world, through Christians' witness, prayer, and service.

*The first resurrection* is referred to in Rev. 20:4-6. The *amillennial* view holds that there are not two resurrections, only one general resurrection of all the dead when Christ comes again. The first resurrection is interpreted to mean that when a Christian dies, he or she is spiritually resurrected and is with Christ. Some people believe that this passage refers especially to the martyrs. While the church continues on earth, the martyrs reign with Christ. Others hold that the first resurrection refers to the time when a person becomes a Christian, for then he or she comes alive in Christ and is seated with him "in the heavenly places" (Eph. 2:6).

*Satan is released* from his prison when the thousand-year period is over (Rev. 20:7-10). Some interpreters believe that, toward the end of the church age, severe trouble and persecution will break out on the earth. Satan will muster all the enemies of the church in a last attempt to eliminate Christianity and defeat Christ. He will deceive nations into believing that he is able to do this. The names *Gog* and *Magog*, taken from Ezekiel 38 and 39, symbolize the enemies of God and his people. Satan will lead his army in a last great onslaught on the "camp of the saints and the beloved city" (Rev. 20:9). Amillennialists do not interpret this literally to mean Jerusalem; they believe it means the last attack on the church.

The battle mentioned here seems to be the battle of Armageddon referred to in Rev. 16:16 and 19:19. Whatever Scripture means by the term *Armageddon* (also spelled *Harmagedon*), it is interesting to note that analysts of world affairs often refer to the possibility of a cataclysmic war as "Armageddon." Writing about all the failures of peace efforts, General Douglas MacArthur stated, "We have had our last chance. If we will not devise some greater and more equitable system, Armageddon will be at the door." Also, in *U.S. News and World Report* following the Persian Gulf war in 1991, an editorial stated that there had been a greater potential for a nuclear disaster than had been supposed. It concluded, "No intelligence service, not even Israel's, suspected that Hussein had gotten as far as he had on the road to Armageddon."

The references to Armageddon in the Revelation do not describe the battle itself. Each concentrates on the victory of Christ. When all the forces of evil—all the antagonists—gather to do battle against Christ and his people, then Christ—the Mighty Warrior—will appear and consume them with the breath of his mouth, with his word of power. Satan then will be thrown into hell, chained forever, never again able to harass and persecute the children of God.

## THE FINAL JUDGMENT (REV. 20:11-15)

Those who interpret chapter 20 literally believe that the judgment at the great white throne is only for the lost and that it will occur after the thousand-year period is over. Others, including amillennialists, believe that all people, both saved and lost, will be included in this judgment. Every person who has ever lived will be resurrected to stand before the judgment seat of Christ.

For Christians, our judgment in relation to our eternal salvation is already past; our names have been written in the Lamb's book of life. Jesus said, "Very truly, I tell you, anyone who hears my word and believes him who sent me has eternal life, and does not come under judgment, but has passed from death to life" (John 5:24). What a comfort to know that we do not have to wait until the judgment day to know whether or not we belong to God! We have the glad certainty right now that we possess eternal life. "Whoever *has* the Son *has* life" (1 John 5:12, italics added). However, on judgment day, a Christian's life will be judged, or evaluated, as to what he or she has done with the life God has given. Passages such as 1 Cor. 3:13-15; 2 Cor. 5:10; and Rev. 20:12 seem to indicate this. Ultimately a person's life-style and what his or her life produces indicates what or who is at the center of that life.

It is interesting to note that "the earth and the heaven fled from [God's] presence" on the throne (Rev. 20:11). Creation, which the sin of Adam and Eve corrupted, also needs to be restored. Paul says that all of creation is on "tiptoe" (*Phillips*, Rom. 8:1-9), waiting for Christ to return. Then it will be released from its bondage to decay and will experience the "freedom of the glory of the children of God" (Rom. 8:21). Creation must be cleansed, renovated, and restored. The apostle Peter says, "The heavens will be set ablaze and dissolved, and the elements will melt with fire[!] But, in accordance with his promise, we wait for new heavens and a new earth, where righteousness is at home" (2 Peter 3:12-13).

All the enemies of Christ and his people are now vanquished. Babylon, the beast, the false prophet, the devil, Death and Hades, and all whose names not written in the "book of life" are thrown into the lake of fire.

## ENCOURAGEMENT AND HOPE

Chapters 19 and 20 echo the keynote of the victory of Jesus Christ, the theme of the Revelation. The Revelation was not written to satisfy curiosity or speculation about the future, but to give courage and hope. The contents of these chapters (19, 20) may puzzle us, but let us remember that Jesus Christ, who will be victorious over every enemy, is coming again to make all things new.

The image of the "great white throne" (20:1) before which we all must stand brings sobering thoughts. How reassuring to have the glad certainty that our names are "written in the book of life" (20:15) and to know that, as we yield our lives to the control of the Holy Spirit, he is at work, bearing fruit through us.

What pain the words *"thrown into the lake of fire"* (20:14) must bring to the loving heart of God. He, who in his love and wisdom had sought to draw people to himself, must now let them experience what they have chosen—complete and eternal exclusion from his presence. O God, stir our hearts with your love and concern for the lost.

Heaven rings with the hallelujahs of victory. When things seem dark and discouraging, let us join in spirit with those victorious songs of heaven and sing, "Praise God! Jesus is victor. He is King of kings and Lord of lords. Hallelujah!"

Alleluia! Sing to Jesus;
His the scepter, his the throne;
Alleluia! His the triumph,
His the victory alone.
Hark! The songs of peaceful Zion
Thunder like a mighty flood.
"Jesus out of every nation
Has redeemed us by his blood."
William Chatterton Dix, 1837–1898

# Lesson 11

## New People in a New World

### REVELATION 21:1—22:5

We should begin this study with a joyous "hallelujah," for now the struggles, sufferings, and judgments are over. Every enemy has been defeated. Christ is King of kings and Lord of lords. We are about to view the celestial city and learn about life in the new heaven and earth.

Think through the Revelation and try to visualize the progression of the book by recalling the name of each chapter or a key idea from each chapter. It would be good if you could also recall the larger divisions of the book. Try to do this without referring to the outline chart.

Read Rev. 21:1—22:5. Then scan Genesis 1–3. On a separate piece of paper, list the contrasts or fulfillments that you find in the following references:

| First Creation | New Creation |
|---|---|
| Genesis: | Revelation: |
| 1:1 | 21:1 |
| 1:5 | 21:25 |
| 1:16 | 21:23 |
| 3:8-10 | 21:3 |
| 3:17 | 22:3 |
| 3:23 | 21:25 |
| 3:24 | 22:14 |

## Study Questions

### REV. 21:1-8: THE NEW HEAVEN AND THE NEW EARTH

1. Read Rev. 21:1-8. What does John see? (vv. 1-2)
   a. What happened to the first heaven and earth? (v. 1) (See also 2 Peter 3:10-13.) What means will God use to restore, purify, and renovate this world?
   b. The new Jerusalem seems to symbolize two things. What are they? (Rev. 21:2, 9-10) The fact that the new Jerusalem comes down from heaven seems to indicate that there will be "heaven on earth"—God's Utopia—in which God's people will dwell.
   c. The meaning of the marriage supper of the Lamb is given in Rev. 21:3. What will be the crowning joy of that event?
2. Which seven evils will be "no more" in the new city? (Rev. 21:1, 4; 22:3, 5) (For the symbolic meaning of the sea [v. 1], see Isa. 57:20 and Rev. 13:1.)
   a. Contrast these "no mores" with the ones listed in Rev. 18:21-23.
   b. Why would the elimination of these evils have special meaning for first-century Christians?
   c. As you contemplate a perfect world, list things you would eliminate from our world today.
3. Who is speaking? (v. 5) What assurance does he give that what he has promised will come to pass? (vv. 5-6)
4. What do the words *"all things new"* mean to you? What do you want made new? What is the meaning of his promise in verses 6-7?
5. Why do you think John interjects the warning in verses 8 and 27? (Remember, John is writing in time, even though he is describing events beyond time.)

### REV. 21:9-27: THE BEAUTIFUL NEW CITY

1. Read Rev. 21:9-27. Note the prominence of the Lamb in the new Jerusalem. Review these earlier references to the Lamb: Rev. 5:12; 6:16; 7:14, 17; 12:11. What do you learn about the Lamb from each of these references?

2. The new Jerusalem, which symbolizes the kingdom of God on earth, is described in terms familiar to John's contemporaries: a city with walls and gates (Rev. 21:12-14). What would the symbolism of this new city's walls and gates suggest to first-century Christians?
3. What words does John use to describe the beauty of the city? (Rev. 21:2, 11)
4. Whose names are on the gates of the city? (Rev. 21:12) Whose names are on the foundations? (Rev. 21:14) What is the symbolic meaning of these names?
5. How is the size of the city portrayed? (vv. 15-17) The city is a perfect cube (Rev. 21:16), as was the Holy of Holies of the Old Testament tabernacle. What may this symbolism suggest?
6. How is the beauty of the city symbolized? (vv. 18-21)
7. Why is there no need for a temple or created lights in the city? (vv. 22-23) What does this reveal about the city?
8. How does John portray the universality, the safety, and the openness of the city? (vv. 24-26)
9. What will guarantee one's residence in the city? (Rev. 21:27b) How may we be sure that our names are in the Lamb's book of life? (See 1 John 5:11-13 and 1 John 1:9.)

## REV. 22:1-5: LIFE IN THE CELESTIAL CITY

1. Read Rev. 22:1-5. In the center of the city is a lovely garden through which a river flows. Note these facts about the river (Rev. 22:1):
   a. What does the river contain? What does it look like? What is its source?
   b. What do these symbolic descriptions tell us about eternal life in the celestial city?
2. Recall what is said about the tree of life in the Garden of Eden (Gen. 3:24). What change has taken place in the garden? (Rev. 22:2) What has caused this change?
3. Life in the new heaven and earth will not be monotonous or boring. It will be filled with meaningful service and joyful worship (Rev. 22:3b). What do you look forward to doing there?

4. Read 1 John 3:2 and then read Rev. 22:4. Close your eyes and meditate on these words: "I will see his face!" What do these words mean to you?

## FOR MEDITATION AND PRAYER

Horatius Bonar, the nineteenth-century author and hymn writer, wrote a book entitled *The Saint's Everlasting Rest.* In it, he suggests that the Christian spend fifteen minutes a day in heaven—being there in thought and contemplation. He promises that doing this will add a new dimension of joy to our Christian experience. The scenes of heaven in the Revelation give us much material on which to meditate. Write a few short prayers of praise and thanksgiving that express your hopes. Share them with your group, if you are studying this book with a group.

As you pray the petition in the Lord's Prayer "Thy kingdom come," remember that these chapters describe that for which you are praying.

# LESSON 11
# NEW PEOPLE IN A NEW WORLD
# REVELATION 21:1—22:5

## Study Helps and Commentary

The consummation—toward which the Revelation and all of history have been progressing—is now before us. Pictured here in symbolic language is the eternal beauty, joy, and blessedness that those who have followed the Lamb will enjoy. These closing chapters are filled with new images, for God has said, "See, I am making all things new" (Rev. 21:5). We see a new heaven and new earth, new Jerusalem, a new people, and a new experience.

## THE NEW HEAVEN AND THE NEW EARTH (REV. 21:1-8)

In the first chapters of Genesis, we read the account of the creation of the world. God made it a beautiful place for human beings, who were the crown of his creation. But when sin came into the world, the results of sin touched all creation. When Christ returns, then, creation will be set free from its bondage to sin and decay (Rom. 8:21). Creation will be restored, renovated, and cleansed to make way for the new creation—the new heaven and earth. What we see in Revelation 21 and 22 is beyond history. It is the experience of all the redeemed after the second coming of Christ, the resurrection, and the judgment.

What a glorious prospect! We will be new people, set free from all the sin, weakness, and limitations that plague us now. We will live in a new world in which all wrong and corruption have been removed. We will live together in love and joy, serving God eternally.

Thomas Torrance, in his book *The Apocalypse Today*, says in relation to this new experience:

> The Garden of Eden meant that God has made man to have communion with him in a perfect environment. Therefore the perfection of the Christian life involves the perfection of earth as well as heaven. The Christian hope is fulfilled only in a new heaven and a new earth peopled with human beings living in holy and loving fellowship with God, with one another, and in harmony with the fulness of creation.[1]

God is planning the very best for his children, and the fulfillment will far surpass our greatest expectations. The reason that the new heaven and earth will be perfect is that God is its author. It originates in heaven (Rev. 21:2). Today people are working hard to improve their world and its environment. Someday this world will be perfected, but only because God makes it so. It will be the perfect, permanent dwelling place of God's redeemed children.

How can we be sure that God is planning such a great future for us? We can be sure because he who has said that he will make all things new is "trustworthy and true" (Rev. 21:5). We can depend on his word. He is the Alpha and the Omega, the beginning and the end. He has created this world with a purpose, and he will bring his plan to completion. He is so certain that his purposes will be accomplished that he can say, "It is done!" (Rev. 21:6). We can be that certain, too.

What a comfort for tested and tried Christians who live in a troubled world! God is in perfect control. He will bring history to an end and will usher in a new world prepared for his own. Therefore, when dark clouds appear on the world's horizon, let us keep this vision before us, knowing that in Christ we have a bright future.

Secular society had pinned its hopes on its own city, Babylon. That has collapsed and is no more. In contrast, we see the heavenly city glorious in beauty—the Holy City, the new Jerusalem—coming down from heaven as a radiant bride adorned for her husband (Rev. 21:2). Earlier (Revelation 19), John described the marriage supper of the Lamb that would soon come. Now, Christ, the heavenly Bridegroom, comes again and is united eternally with his bride, the church.

The city John describes here is not to be understood as the literal, earthly city of Jerusalem. John goes beyond that. In the spirit, he is given a vision of the heavenly Jerusalem, the place where Jesus said he would go to prepare for his own. John is using earthly language to help us understand the glory of the heavenly city. There is a mystery as to what the new Jerusalem will be like, just as we do not understand what our resurrection bodies will be like. But nonetheless, the heavenly Jerusalem will be a reality.

As John views the heavenly city from the top of a high mountain, he tells us in symbolic language what the city is like. The first thing he notices is that *it is a city of light.* The glory of God emanates from it so that it shines with "a radiance like a very rare jewel" (Rev. 21:11). God's presence fills the city with light, which should not surprise us because John says, "God is light and in him there is no darkness at all" (1 John 1:5). Now that sin has been removed, God can dwell with his people and have perfect fellowship with them (Rev. 21:3). When God created the first world, he made the sun, moon, and stars to provide its light. Here, in his new creation, there is no longer any need for the sun and moon, "for the glory of God is its light, and its lamp is the Lamb" (Rev. 21:23).

*The city has order, balance, and security,* as symbolized by the walls and gates (Rev. 21:12-13). There is no fear of exclusion and there is perfect security.

*The city is founded on the word of God,* that word which the Old Testament prophets and the New Testament apostles proclaimed. This word is symbolized by the names of the twelve tribes of Israel inscribed on the gates and the names of the twelve apostles on the foundation stones (Rev. 21:12-14). These foundations are unshakable; this city will last forever.

*This city is large and spacious.* There is room for all who would enter, symbolized by its measurements: twelve thousand stadia (1,500 miles) long, wide, and high (Rev. 21:16). This number is a product of three (God's number, the Trinity) multiplied by four (number of the earth or universe) times one thousand (the number of completeness). This symbolic number thus indicates the vastness of the heavenly city and also that God's redemption has touched the whole universe.

*The heavenly city is a place of exquisite beauty and radiance* (Rev. 21:18-21). It seems as if John is groping for words to describe its splendor. The cube, which symbolizes the city's symmetry and perfection, is made of pure gold, transparent as glass (Rev. 21:18). Can you imagine transparent gold, or picture the glory of God that fills the city shining out through the gold? The wall of the city is built of jasper, a precious stone. This city needs no wall to protect it from enemies, as did the ancient cities of John's day. But he is using an ancient city as a model to convey an image of the heavenly city.

Picture a wall built of jasper, its foundation adorned with precious stones; every gate is a huge single pearl; the streets are made of pure, transparent gold—and all of this reflects, radiates, and enhances the glory of God that fills the city! John has graphically revealed to us the beauty, glory, radiance, and perfection of this eternal city.

*This city is for the whole world* (Rev. 21:24-26). In John 3:16, we read, "For God so loved the world that he gave his only Son, so that everyone who believes in him may not perish [not be excluded from the eternal city] but may have eternal life." This is an international city, for the nations "walk by its light, and the kings of the earth . . . bring their glory into it." This city will include Christians from every nation, tribe, and tongue—all whose names are written in the Lamb's book of life.

## LIFE IN THE CELESTIAL CITY (REV. 22:1-5)

*The city is vibrant with life from the eternal God* (Rev. 22:1-2). In the center of the city—the city square—are a river and a tree. The river, bright as crystal, flows "from the throne of God and of the

Lamb," symbolizing eternal life that has its source in God. Concerning the life Jesus gives, he said, " 'Let anyone who is thirsty, come to me, and . . . drink. . . .' Out of the believer's heart shall flow rivers of living water" (John 7:37-38).

The life we now experience in Christ is dynamic, vibrant, and growing. In eternity, too, our spiritual lives will not stagnate. They will continue to flow and grow because God's life is in us. This life is not fixed so that it can never change, like unchangeable granite. Rather, eternal life is full of vitality and is constantly being renewed. Youth, too, will last forever, for through our communion with Christ, who is Life, we will be constantly recreated.

In the first garden that God created, two trees had specific significance: the tree of life and the tree of the knowledge of good and evil. After Adam and Eve disobeyed God by eating from the forbidden tree, God barred them from access to the tree of life, lest their alienation from him be fixed forever. But now, in this new garden, we see the tree of life again. The Greek expression for this is "the wood of life." Hence, this tree symbolizes the cross—the salvation that Jesus won for us by pouring out his life on that tree. Throughout eternity, the presence of "the wood of life" will cause our hearts to praise and thank him that his death made it possible for us to have a part in this beautiful city of life.

The tree of life mentioned in Rev. 22:2 bears fruit constantly, and its leaves "are for the healing of the nations." The children of Adam and Eve are no longer barred from eating of the tree. We can partake freely of its fruits, which symbolize the very life of Christ that will sustain and nourish us throughout eternity. The fruit of the tree of life now heals all the fruits of sin.

*Absent from the beautiful city* are elements and conditions that plague us now and keep us from experiencing perfect peace and joy. The absence of these conditions makes the heavenly city a glorious place of perfection. Notice the conditions that will not be present in the beautiful city:

*No more tears* (Rev. 21:4). As a mother stoops down and wipes the tears from her child's eyes, so God will wipe every tear from our eyes. There will be no more heartaches and disappointments that cause tears.

*No more death.* Separation because of death causes tears and sorrow, mourning and crying. But now death is eliminated, so there will be no more separation, only a joyful, eternal companionship with those we love.

*No more pain.* What a blessed prospect this is for those who in this life have had to learn to live with pain, or for Christians who were tortured to the point of death! We will be free from pain forever—both physically and mentally.

*No more thirst* (Rev. 21:6b). There will be no more restless longings for something to satisfy the deep needs of the human heart. Jesus, we recall, said to the Samaritan woman, "Those who drink of the water that I will give them will never be thirsty" (John 4:14). Even now, we Christians experience a deep inner contentment, but we also long for a deeper and more meaningful experience with Christ. In the new Jerusalem, all these longings will be met. We will know Christ in all his fullness and continue to drink from the fountain of the water of life—which is Christ himself.

*No more darkness.* "There will be no night there" (Rev. 21:25; 22:5). In our cities today, the darkness of night often causes people to fear crime and molestation. But all darkness and accompanying fears will be eliminated from the eternal city. There will be no need for artificial lighting or for created luminaries, for God himself will light the city (Rev. 22:5).

*No more of anything accursed* (Rev. 22:3). When sin came into the world, the curse of sin touched all creation. The ground was cursed; thorns and thistles sprang up, and Adam and Eve and their progeny were destined to make their bread by the sweat of their face (Gen. 3:14). Throughout our lives, we are plagued by struggle and frustration. All that will be over, however, in the new city of God. The curse of sin will have been removed forever. We will be set free to serve God perfectly in the service of worship. There will be no boredom in the heavenly city, only ceaseless, joyful activity.

Notice who will be excluded from the new Jerusalem (Rev. 21:8, 27):

*The cowardly.* These did not have the courage or strength to remain faithful to Jesus during suffering and persecution.

*The faithless.* This term may refer to those who gave up their faith in Jesus when tested by trials or those who never put their faith and trust fully in Christ.

*The polluted.* These people contaminated themselves by worshiping the beast and became ensnared by the enticements of the worldly city, Babylon.

*Murderers and fornicators.* "Murderers" may refer to those who persecuted and killed Christians or to murderers in general. "Fornicators" may refer to those who committed spiritual adultery with the whore, Babylon, or it may refer to impurity in general.

*Sorcerers and idolaters.* These are the people whose religion was centered in the occult, witchcraft, astrology, or magic. Idolatry, by definition, is putting anything in the place of God.

*Liars.* These were involved in any kind of falsehood, phoniness, hypocrisy, and/or insincerity. God is a God of truth and hates falsehood.

*The unclean or anyone who practices abomination.* There will be no unholiness in the new Jerusalem.

Let us remember that God can and will forgive all these sins. We are all sinners, but the people mentioned here are excluded from the glory of the eternal city because they refused to humble themselves and seek God's gift of forgiveness in Christ. Therefore, they must experience the second death—spiritual death—which is exclusion from the presence of God forever, from all that is good, beautiful, true, joyful, and glorious. What a tragedy! Yet we can see the mercy of God even here, for heaven would be like hell for these people. Jesus is the center of heaven, and only those who love him will enjoy his presence. The enemies of God would be most miserable in his holy presence.

## THE CROWNING GLORY OF THIS NEW EXPERIENCE

Our crowning glory will be living in the very presence of Christ and having unbroken, perfect fellowship with him. The greatest joy in our Christian experience now is to sense the nearness of Christ and to find joy in his presence. But so often, this experience fluctuates. In the heavenly home, Christ's presence will be constant. There will be nothing to mar this fellowship, no cloud to hide his glorious face. He will live in the midst of his people. "They will be his peoples, and God himself will be with them" (Rev. 21:3). The apostle John also wrote, "Beloved, we are God's children now; what we will be has not yet been revealed. What we do know is this: when he is revealed, we will be like him, for we will see him as he is" (1 John 3:2). We "will see his face, and his name will be on . . . [our] foreheads" (Rev. 22:4). Christ will be the center of our thoughts, our love, our joy.

Worship will be perfected in the heavenly city. The temple, with its sacrificial system, was of great importance in Jewish worship. The chief function of the church today is to assist us in our worship of God, whether in prayer, praise, or service. In the heavenly Jerusalem, however, there will be no need for a temple (Rev. 21:22), for God and the Lamb are the temple. We will need nothing to assist us in our worship, for we will have direct access to God; the "gates will never be shut" (Rev. 21:25). Paul writes,

"No eye has seen, nor ear heard,
Nor the human heart conceived,
what God has prepared for those who love him."
(1 Corinthians 2:9)

Jerusalem the golden,
With milk and honey blest,
Beneath your contemplation
Sink heart and voice oppressed.
I know not, oh, I know not,
What social joys are there,
What radiancy of glory,
What bliss beyond compare.

Oh, sweet and blessed country,
The home of God's elect!
Oh, sweet and blessed country,
That eager hearts expect!
In mercy, Jesus bring us
To that dear land of rest!
You are, with God the Father
And Spirit, ever blest.

Bernard of Cluny, 12th century
Tr. John Mason Neale, 1818–1866

# Lesson 12

## He Is Coming Soon

### REVELATION 22:6-21

The Revelation focuses on Christ—his victory and his coming. Think through the book with the following guidelines in mind. What picture of Christ do you get from this book? Notice how he is presented. Think about the meaning of the many names he is called. Review his role and activities. In what ways has this study made a difference in your view of Christ?

The Revelation presents a striking contrast between those who follow the Lamb and those who follow the beast. Try to recall the contrasts between these two groups, in terms of the object of their worship, their goals, and their ultimate end, and whatever other contrasts you can see. Use a separate piece of paper.

*Followers of the Lamb* *Followers of the Beast*

### Study Questions

#### THE AUTHENTICITY OF THE MESSAGE OF THE REVELATION

1. The angel says to John in Rev. 22:6, "These words are trustworthy and true." Read Rev. 22:6-21 to find assurances that the message of the book is reliable and true. Note especially verses 6b, 8, and 16.
2. Has your study of the Revelation and these assurances of its reliability changed your outlook on this book? If so, how?

#### THE IMPORTANCE OF THE MESSAGE OF THE REVELATION

1. What instruction is given to John? (v. 10)
   a. Why do you think it is important that his book remain open for people to study?

b. What warning and encouragement does verse 11 hold?

2. What warning is given in verses 18-19?
   a. What things in this book might a person be tempted to "take away"? Why would doing this be such a serious offense?
   b. What might a person try to add to this book?

## THE CLAIMS OF CHRIST

In each of the following verses, note who is speaking and the claim made:

| | *Who Speaks* | *Claim—"I am . . ."* |
|---|---|---|
| 22:12-13 | | |
| 21:5-6 | | |
| 1:8 | | |
| 1:17b | | |

1. How do these verses show that Jesus claims to be true God?
2. Why is it important to believe that Jesus is the true God?
3. Note the terms Jesus uses to describe himself in Rev. 22:16b. What claim is he making by this reference to David?
4. The morning star heralds the rising of the sun and the breaking of a new day. What is Jesus affirming when he refers to himself as "the bright morning star"?

## THE SEVEN BEATITUDES IN THE REVELATION

*Beatitude* comes from a Latin word meaning "blessedness." We are familiar with the Beatitudes spoken by Jesus in Matt. 5:1-11. In each of the following references, note which conditions make us ready to receive the sevenfold blessing.

1:3
14:13
16:15
19:9
20:6
22:7b
22:14

1. The sixth beatitude (Rev. 22:7b) promises a blessing to those who "keep" the words of this book. To "keep" involves the total person,

mind, emotion, and will. How has the study of this book influenced or blessed you in each of these areas?

2. What has this study motivated you to *do*?
3. The seventh beatitude (22:14) assures that those who wash their robes ["keep on washing" in the Greek] will enter the celestial city. What is meant by "robes," and how are they cleansed? (See 1 John 1:7, 9.)

## THE GRACIOUS INVITATION TO COME TO CHRIST

1. What is the condition for coming to Christ? (22:17b)
   a. What are some indications that a person is thirsty for the water of life?
   b. How do we drink the water of life? (See Rev. 3:20 and John 7:37-39.)
   c. As a response to Jesus' gracious invitation, pray this prayer by Martin Luther.

      O dearest Jesus, holy child,
      Prepare a bed, soft, undefiled,
      A holy shrine, within my heart,
      That you and I need never part.
2. What is John's response to Jesus' promise to come again? (Rev. 22:20b)
   a. How do you feel about his coming again? Do you wish Jesus would hurry his coming, or would you rather that he delay a while? Why?
   b. How will you incorporate your study of the Revelation into your life from now on?

## PRAISE AND THANKSGIVING

Close your study with prayers of praise and thanksgiving for the blessings that the message of the Revelation has brought to you. Write out your prayers and pray them. If you are studying with a group, pray them together.

Sing joyfully that great song of faith, "How Firm a Foundation," which expresses the message of the Revelation so meaningfully. Or listen to some of the glorious music from *The Messiah*.

Read aloud in unison the benediction of Rev. 22:20-21.

## POSTSCRIPT

May the promised blessings of this book continue to abide with us until faith becomes sight, when we will see Christ and one another in the beautiful city of God and forever sing praises to our Lamb.

## LESSON 12
## HE IS COMING SOON
## REVELATION 22:6-21

### Study Helps and Commentary

We have now come to the last segment in the Revelation, the epilogue. In the preceding lesson, we viewed the beautiful, eternal city that awaits all who love God and have been faithful to the Lamb. We see everything that was lost in the first paradise in Eden being restored in the second paradise of the heavenly Jerusalem.

The visions that were given to John are over. Before he closes his book, however, he seeks to impress certain truths upon his readers. These truths come to us through three voices—that of an angel, of John, and of Jesus. At times, it is difficult to determine who is speaking. Perhaps this is because we are to realize that, regardless of who speaks, it is really the voice of Jesus that comes to us through the whole book.

### THE AUTHENTICITY OF THE MESSAGE OF THE REVELATION

The angel affirms the genuineness of the book, saying that the words of the Revelation are trustworthy and true because they have come from God himself. He is the One who has guided "the spirits of the prophets" (Rev. 22:6). John is repeating here what he said at the outset of the book: God is the author.

Next, John verifies the fact that it was he who had received these visions (Rev. 22:8). Well known to the churches in Asia Minor, John could be trusted.

Finally, Jesus himself attests to the validity of the contents of the Revelation. He sent his angel with the message to the churches (Rev. 22:16). He testifies that all the things that have been written are true (Rev. 22:20).

# THE IMPORTANCE OF THE MESSAGE OF THE REVELATION

The Revelation is not to be sealed up because "the time is near" (Rev. 22:10). It is to remain open so that it can be read, for its message is always contemporary. While the Revelation grew out of the difficult situation in which the first-century Christians found themselves—a situation where emperor worship was demanded at the threat of death—this book contains a message for Christians in any period of history. Therefore, the time is always near. We must ever heed the message of this book: to be loyal to Christ no matter what the cost.

Rev. 22:11 points to the seriousness of rejecting the message of Christ. It has been said, "The same sun that hardens bricks melts butter." Our relationship with Christ depends on our willful response to him. Each time a person says no to the appeal of Christ, a process of hardening sets in. If a person continues to say no, a time may come when he or she cannot say yes. Christ does not force anyone to follow him. He respects the dignity of the human will. Thus we read, "Let the evildoer still do evil, and the filthy still be filthy" (22:11).

Everyone is free to make his or her own choice, but one day that choice will become unchangeable. Then those who have refused to honor Christ will be found outside the gates of the heavenly city (Rev. 22:15), in the company of all others who have loved their own way of life and have refused to receive the love of Christ. The greatest tragedy is that on that day they will no longer have the opportunity to repent; they will face eternal exclusion from the presence of Christ.

By the same token, each time people surrender to the promptings of the Holy Spirit and say yes to Christ, their relationship with Christ becomes more firm so that the righteous will "still do right, and the holy still be holy" (22:11)—until that day.

Those who study the Revelation have always been tempted to set dates, make dogmatic predictions, and view contemporary world events as positive fulfillment of the Revelation. This book, however, was not written to provide material for wild speculations. There is another danger, too, for some people will shun this book altogether, denying its importance or its divine authorship. The warning in Rev. 22:18-19 is directed against those who add to or take away from the words of this prophecy. It may also refer to those who manipulate this book to make it fit their own particular schemes of eschatology. The severity of the judgment described in these verses impresses on the reader the seriousness of tampering with this book.

## THE SEVEN BEATITUDES IN THE REVELATION

The Revelation contains seven beatitudes. Note some of their differences. The first one promises a blessing for those who read, hear, and keep what is written in this prophecy (Rev. 1:3). Other beatitudes encourage Christians to persevere during difficult times.

The last two beatitudes are stated in the final segment of the book. The sixth is directed to the individual—not to the church as a whole, but to the "one who keeps the words of the prophecy of this book" (Rev. 22:7b). The seventh speaks of the blessedness of those who have washed "their robes" so that they are ready and prepared for the heavenly city (Rev. 22:14).

God has provided, in Christ, all we need to wash our robes. Through his death and resurrection, Christ has offered forgiveness and salvation to all. But as William Barclay says in his commentary, "Man has to wash his own robes in the blood of Jesus Christ." That is, we must confess, repent, and accept God's forgiveness. We must also appropriate all that God has done for us by opening our hearts to Christ (Rev. 3:20). When Jesus said, "I am the bread of life" (John 6:35), he indicated that he is to be "eaten"—assimilated into all of life. When we possess the indwelling life of Christ, we are prepared to enter the heavenly city through the gates.

## THE GRACIOUS INVITATION TO COME TO CHRIST

The message in the Revelation is urgent. Three times in the closing verses, Jesus says, "I am coming soon" (Rev. 22:7, 12, 20), implying that he may come at any time. The first-century Christians looked for him to come in their generation. Because he has delayed his coming so long, many tend to overlook this great event or to say, as did the scoffers in Peter's day, "Where is the promise of his coming? For ever since our ancestors died, all things continue as they were from the beginning of creation" (2 Peter 3:3-4). Peter then reminds his readers that Christ is delaying his coming because he is patient, "not wanting any to perish, but all to come to repentance" (2 Peter 3:9).

Jesus sounds this same note of urgency in the Gospels when he says, "Keep awake therefore, for you do not know on what day your Lord is coming. . . . Therefore you also must be ready, for the Son of Man is coming at an unexpected hour" (Matt. 24:42, 44). The appearance of the heavenly Bridegroom is the event for which his bride, the church, is longing and waiting. Therefore, we should respond, "Come, Lord Jesus!"

The invitation to come to Christ is open to all (Rev. 22:17). In view of the judgments that will fall on those who reject Christ and the blessings that are in store for those who love Christ, John cannot close without extending a final appeal to all those who have not made use of the present opportunity to come to Christ. Christ has not yet come; the door of salvation is still open. When he returns, the opportunity to enter the gates will end. "The Spirit and the bride say, 'Come.' " The Holy Spirit, through the word and preachers of that word, says, "Come." Through its witnessing, the bride—the church—says, "Come." All who have heard and responded say, "Come."

What are the requisites for accepting this invitation? *To be thirsty, to desire the water of life,* and *to take it freely.* Isaiah calls out the same invitation when he says, "Ho, everyone who thirsts, come to the waters; and you that have no money, come, buy and eat!" (Isa. 55:1). What simple requirements these are, and yet how profound!

*First, people need to thirst,* to sense a spiritual need and an inner vacuum that only the Spirit can fill.

*Next, people need to desire the water of life,* to want Christ and believe that he can satisfy the deep longings of the human heart. The world provides a variety of ways through which people seek to fill this vacuum, but people must reject these ways and be willing to explore Christ's way.

*Finally, people need to take the water of life.* They must come boldly to Christ, open up to him, and appropriate his very life so that it can fill their total being. All who have heeded this gracious invitation are ready for his coming. Thus, they can say together, with the Spirit and the bride, "Come, Lord Jesus," and live in joyful expectation of his coming.

## TRUTHS TO BE TREASURED

We have come to the end of our study of the Revelation. As you think through the book, you will want to remember certain truths and highlights. Perhaps these questions will assist in impressing these highlights on your heart:

1. Has your view or concept of Christ been enlarged?

Have you seen Christ in all his resurrection glory, holding the destiny of the world in his hands, maintaining perfect control of history, conquering every enemy, and finally bringing history to a close as he returns as the victorious King of kings and Lord of lords? Have you seen him as the concerned Friend, walking in the midst of his church, encouraging, exhorting, warning? Have you seen him as the Lamb, who is in reality the Shepherd, who comforts his persecuted children and leads them home where he will live in fellowship with them in the new Jerusalem?

2. Have you understood the meaning of true worship?

We have seen that the worship of heaven is joyful and directed to the triune God. It is full of praise for all that God is. It is full of thanksgiving for all that God has done in his work of creation and redemption. It is full of love for Jesus, who gave his life that we might have life. It grows out of the word of God, is Spirit produced, and fills the heart with song.

We see, too, that true worship may flow from an anguished heart that cries, "How long, O Lord?" It may flow from a heart that may not even be able to find words, from someone who can only express a deep groan from the depths of the spirit. Surely this must have been the case in the lives of the many persecuted and martyred Christians. True worship, then, takes place when the hearts of human beings reach out to the heart of God, whether in joy or in sorrow.

3. Have you become aware of the many hymns and other great music inspired by the Revelation?

Find, for example, the following themes from *The Messiah*: "Behold the Lamb of God" (Revelation 5); "But who may abide the day of his coming? And who shall stand when he appeareth? He is like a refiner's fire" (this theme runs throughout the series of judgments in Revelation 6, 8, 9, and 16); "For unto us a child is born" (Revelation 12); the "Hallelujah Chorus" (Rev. 11:15; 19:1-6); and the final chorus from *The Messiah*, "Worthy Is the Lamb," "Blessing and Honor," and the final "Amen" (Revelation 5). Many masterpieces of art have also been inspired by the Revelation.

4. Have the sufferings and trials depicted in the Revelation caused you to examine the quality of your own faith? Do you want to be more

loyal to Christ, no matter what the cost, knowing that loyalty to him means triumph now and forever?

5. Have you become more aware of the role that Satan plays in the world scene and of the subtle ways by which he tries to influence people to follow "Babylon"?

Have you been encouraged to know that the devil is a defeated enemy and that through your union with Christ, you also have victory over him? (Remember Rev. 12:11.)

6. Has your heart been gripped and burdened by the realization that many people have refused to follow the Lamb and have been seduced by the wiles of the whore, Babylon, and therefore will have to suffer the terrible judgments of the wrath of God and be shut out forever from the beautiful city of God?

Will you tell them that the door is still open? Will you urge them to "drink of the water of life" while there is still time?

7. Does the vision of the new heaven and earth fill your heart with joy, expectation, and longing for the day when you will stand in the presence of Jesus, rejoicing in all the beauty and glory that he has prepared for you, and living in fellowship with him and with one another eternally?

When he says, "I am coming soon," does your heart respond eagerly, "Come, Lord Jesus"?

"The grace of the Lord Jesus be with all the saints. Amen."

Our hope and expectation,
O Jesus, now appear;
Arise O Sun so longed for,
O'er this benighted sphere!

With hearts and hands uplifted,
We plead, O Lord, to see
The day of earth's redemption
That brings us unto thee!

Laurentius Laurentii, 1660–1722
Tr. Sarah Borthwick Findlater, 1823–1907

## For Further Study


Barclay, William. *The Revelation of John*, vols. 1 and 2. Philadelphia: Westminster/John Knox, 1976.

Efird, James M. *Revelation for Today*. Nashville: Abingdon, 1989.

Hughes, Philip Edgcumbe. *The Book of Revelation: A Commentary*. Grand Rapids: Eerdmans, 1990.

Krodel, Gerhard A. *Augsburg Commentary on the New Testament: Revelation*. Minneapolis: Augsburg, 1981.

Morris, Leon. *Revelation* (Tyndale New Testament Commentaries). Grand Rapids: Eerdmans, 1987.

Mounce, Robert H. *What Are We Waiting For?: A Commentary on Revelation*. Grand Rapids: Eerdmans, 1977.

# Endnotes

*Introduction*

1. See Julian P. Love, *How to Read the Bible* (New York: Macmillan, 1959), and Donald W. Richardson, *The Revelation of Jesus Christ* (Louisville, Ky.: Westminster/John Knox Press, 1964).
2. Leon Morris, *Apocalyptic* (Grand Rapids: Eerdmans, 1972).

*Lesson 1*

1. William Hendricksen, *More Than Conquerors* (Grand Rapids: Baker Book House, 1975).
2. Hanns Lilje, *The Last Book of the Bible* (Philadelphia: Fortress Press, 1957).

*Lesson 2*

1. Lilje, *The Last Book of the Bible.*
2. M. Basilea Schlink, *World in Revolt* (Minneapolis: Bethany Fellowship, 1969).
3. William Barclay, *The Revelation of John*, vol. 1 (Philadelphia: Westminster, 1959).
4. W. M. Ramsey (London: Hodder, Stoughton, 1904).

*Lesson 3*

1. George Eldon Ladd, *A Commentary on the Revelation of John* (Grand Rapids: Eerdmans, 1972).
2. Hendricksen, *More Than Conquerors.*
3. Ladd, *Commentary on the Revelation.*
4. Barclay, *Revelation of John*, vol. 1.
5. G. B. Caird, *The Revelation of St. John the Divine* (New York: Harper, 1966).

*Lesson 4*

1. Lilje, *Last Book of the Bible.*
2. Barclay, *Revelation of John*, vol. 2, 20.
3. Thomas F. Torrance, *The Apocalypse Today* (Grand Rapids: Eerdmans, 1957).

4. Leon Morris, *The Revelation of St. John* (Grand Rapids: Eerdmans, 1987).
5. Ladd, *Commentary on the Revelation.*

*Lesson 5*
1. Morris, *The Revelation of St. John.*
2. Isbon T. Beckwith, *The Apocalypse of John* (Grand Rapids: Eerdmans, 1967).

*Lesson 6*
1. Lilje, *Last Book of the Bible.*
2. Ibid.
3. Russell Chandler, *Racing Toward 2001* (Grand Rapids: Zondervan, 1992).

*Lesson 7*
1. Torrance, *Apocalypse Today.*
2. Lilje, *Last Book of the Bible.*

*Lesson 8*
1. Merrill C. Tenney, *Interpreting Revelation* (Grand Rapids: Eerdmans, 1957).

*Lesson 9*
1. Beckwith, *Apocalypse of John.*

*Lesson 11*
1. Torrance, *Apocalypse Today.*

*Lesson 12*
1. Barclay, *Revelation of John*, vol. 2.